Atlas of
Ancient Civilizations

Illustrations by
Gerry Embleton

Maps by Geographical Projects London

Atlas of Ancient Civilizations

Keith Branigan

Heinemann London

Geographical Director **Shirley Carpenter**
Editor **M. H. Chandler**
Art Director **Roger Hyde**
Research **Marian Berman**

William Heinemann Ltd., 15–16 Queen Street, London W1X 8BE
London   Melbourne   Toronto
Johannesburg   Auckland

Printed in Spain by TONSA - San Sebastián - Dep. Legal: S.S. 812/75

Contents

Introduction 7

Chapter 1 Before Civilization 8

2 Early Civilization in Mesopotamia 18

3 The Civilization of the Nile Valley 28

4 The Civilization of the Indus Valley 42

5 The Civilization of Northern China 50

6 Maritime Civilizations of the Mediterranean 60

7 The Great Empires of Western Asia 72

8 The Civilization of Greece 84

9 The Civilization of Rome 96

10 Early Civilizations of America 110

Epilogue 122

Index 124

Introduction

ATLAS OF ANCIENT CIVILIZATIONS, paradoxically enough, is essentially a book about *modern* men and women— about people seeking to better themselves, planning for the future, following and creating fashions, improving their technologies, improvising art forms and stretching out for a better understanding of their world. The paradox is unavoidable, for innovation, creativity and forward planning, far from being the exclusive preserves of our own time, were the major driving forces behind the ancient civilizations of Mesopotamia, Egypt, China, Greece and Rome.

The author begins by examining the modes of human existence that preceded, and gradually led up to, civilized living. He puts forward a definition of civilization closely similar to that once given by those profound social and economic historians J. L. and Barbara Hammond: *Civilization implies that man has learnt to mould his surroundings to his own purposes; that he is not in complete subjection to nature or even just holding his own in a stern struggle.*

To have reached that stage at all means that man must have evolved tools, technologies and techniques far beyond the primitive; and he is likely to have evolved them on different lines in different places. Once he has learnt to mould his surroundings, his purposes include far more than merely satisfying his hunger. His mind turns to art, religion, literature, law and justice, philosophy and social organization. All these things, too, will take on a different shape in different regions, a shape often strongly influenced, though never wholly dictated, by climate and terrain.

This book looks first at the highly diverse civilizations that grew up in the valleys of the Euphrates, the Nile, the Indus and China's Yellow river; next at the maritime civilizations of the Mediterranean and at the great empires of the broad lands of western Asia; then at the magnificent civilizations of Greece and Rome and finally at the amazing civilizations that developed in the comparative isolation of the pre-Columban New World.

The full-colour maps accurately set the geographical and historical scene for each civilization; the carefully researched artwork reconstructions and photographs bring visual immediacy to the past; and the concise, lucid text accords to our forefathers the same human understanding as we try to extend to our contemporaries.

1 Before Civilization

To day man's use of science and technology has created complex and advanced civilizations in most parts of the world. Living in one of these civilizations, we can very easily forget that man has been a civilized creature for only a fraction of the time he has lived on earth. The earliest civilizations we know of first appeared between five and six thousand years ago; the earliest recognizable remains of man (the species *Homo habilis*) are some two million or more years old. In our modern world, with its tremendous pace of invention and discovery, it is difficult to appreciate how slowly our forebears progressed towards a civilized state. Yet during the slow-moving two million years before civilization, some of the most important developments and discoveries in the whole history of mankind took place.

Man belongs to one of the families within the order *Primates*—the highest order of mammals. But he differs greatly from the other primates in his upright stance, the dexterity of his hands, and, above all, in his superior brain, which gives him so many of his advantages over other animals. Even the earliest men to leave traces of their existence used their brains and their hands to produce simple stone tools which gave them an advantage over other creatures. From their first pebble choppers the hand axe proper eventually developed, and in time this was followed by a whole range of more specialized tools, first of stone, later of bone and antler.

The development of Stone Age man's tool kit underlines one of humanity's most important abilities—that of learning from experience. A major step in this process was the development of speech, which enabled a man to exchange ideas with his fellows. Thereafter, people could learn not only from their own experience but also from the experiences of others.

Slowly the resulting new skills and new ideas spread throughout Africa, Asia and Europe. One of the most important was

Men of the Old Stone Age took a great step forward when they first learned to erect artificial shelters where no natural ones, such as caves, existed. These mammoth hunters of south Russia made their shelters by using mammoth tusks, and sometimes branches, to support a roof of skins.

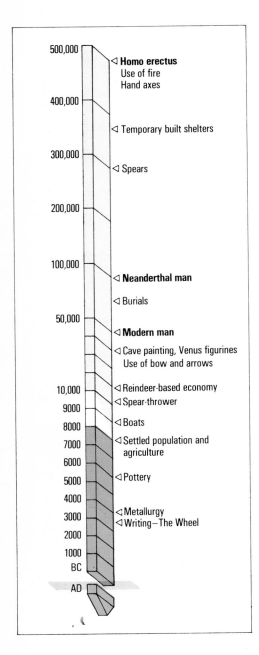

500,000 ◁ **Homo erectus**
Use of fire
Hand axes

400,000

◁ Temporary built shelters

300,000

◁ Spears

200,000

100,000

◁ **Neanderthal man**

◁ Burials

50,000

◁ **Modern man**

◁ Cave painting, Venus figurines
Use of bow and arrows

10,000 ◁ Reindeer-based economy
9000 ◁ Spear-thrower
8000 ◁ Boats
7000 ◁ Settled population and
agriculture
6000
5000 ◁ Pottery
4000
3000 ◁ Metallurgy
◁ Writing—The Wheel
2000
1000
BC

AD

In the beginning man's only great advantages over other animals were his better brain and more useful hands. This chart shows the major landmarks on his long march towards civilization, achieved by his use of both.

Even to think of shaping stones into tools and weapons must have called for foresight and imagination. To develop the skill to do so really well demanded ages of experience. Tools, from left to right, are a chopper of 500,000 B.C., a hand axe of between 250,000 and 200,000 B.C., and a fine, well-made arrowhead of around 20,000 B.C.

the use of fire, perhaps first discovered by Peking Man *(Homo erectus pekinensis)* who inhabited northern China half a million years ago. Another was the idea of erecting an artificial shelter where natural ones, such as caves, were lacking. The most interesting of these early shelters to survive seem to have been tentlike structures with their floors sunk slightly below ground level and their roofs made of skins supported by mammoth tusks. The remains of several such structures have been found in eastern Europe and Russia. The quantity of mammoth tusks employed in them was often considerable and gives a very misleading impression of the food sources of the people who built them. Men of that time certainly hunted mammoth, but, depending on which part of the world they lived in, they also successfully hunted elephant, rhinoceros, wild ox, deer, horse, and bear, as well as many smaller animals.

To help them, Paleolithic (Old Stone Age) hunters hit on the idea of extending the reach of the human arm by using sticks tipped with points of stone. In other words, they developed the spear. The earliest spears, so far known, date to about 300,000 B.C. They were made entirely of wood and rarely survived, but one of later date has been found, still in position between the ribs of a mammoth, near Hanover in Germany, proving how effective they were. The introduction, still later, of finely worked flint spearheads increased the killing power of the Stone Age spear, and both the range and penetration of the spear were further improved by the invention of the spear thrower. By that time, the hunters had also improved their armoury by inventing the bow, which, with its long range and speed of discharge, made it easier to hunt down animals that were both swift and wary.

The invention of the bow coincides broadly with the change-over in Europe from an economy based on hunting a variety of animals to one based mainly on the reindeer. Towards the close of the last Ice Age, between 15,000 and 9000 B.C., the reindeer herds that roamed Europe south of the retreating ice sheet were intensively and systematically exploited. They provided not only meat but also skins, sinews, bone and antler, for

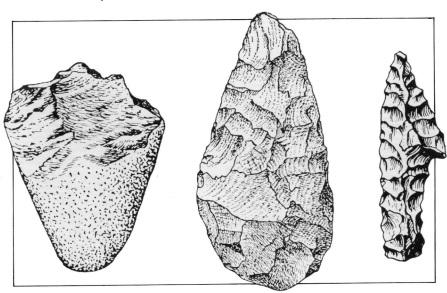

clothing, thread, lines, tools, weapons and ornaments. Rubbish deposits found on the sites where some of the reindeer hunters lived show that some groups depended on the reindeer for over 90 per cent of these commodities. So it is not surprising that before the Ice Age ended some groups of hunters had begun to follow the seasonal migrations of individual reindeer herds, thus taking the first step towards the domestication of animals. At the same time man seems to have realized that there were certain advantages—particularly in hunting—in combining forces with other men.

From this time on, cave paintings in northern Spain and southern France show not one or two but literally dozens of men involved in organized hunts. Some men act as beaters while others wait in a line to shoot the animals as they break cover. The same series of paintings also shows the first pictures of human warfare.

The spear thrower, invented towards the close of the last Ice Age, greatly increased the range and penetration of the spear by providing an artificial extension to the hunter's throwing arm. Scarcely changed, it has remained in use among Eskimos and Australian Aborigines to our own time.

The maximum extent of the icecaps that covered much of northern Asia, Europe and North America during the time man was moving towards a settled way of life. This map shows also the four river valleys where civilization took shape after the icecaps' final retreat.

Geographical Projects

These particular paintings were preceded, in the same areas, by many others, the earliest of which date back to about 40,000 B.C. No one is sure why these superb paintings of wild animals were made—often in the deepest and most inaccessible parts of a cave. But they show very clearly that man had now developed the ability to express in visual form what he felt about the world around him. They also suggest that he had developed certain beliefs about the relationship between himself and the world he lived in, and how that relationship might be changed to his advantage. He had in fact begun to develop a religion and a belief in supernatural powers. The first signs of religious beliefs are to be found among Neanderthal man, who sometimes buried his dead in proper graves, occasionally with grave offerings—things of the kind the dead man may once have used. At Mount Carmel in Palestine a cemetery of ten such burials suggests that there it was already quite a regular practice.

There is also evidence suggesting that as religious beliefs developed, certain men were selected to intercede with the supernatural on behalf of their fellows—to practise magic for them. In the region of the Arièges river, in France, there is a famous cave painting of a "sorcerer" wearing an antler mask, while from Starr Carr in Yorkshire, England, archaeologists have actually recovered such a mask. The "sorcerers" were possibly the world's first specialists, men at least partly supported by other members of their tribe or community so that they could devote themselves to their special skills and tasks.

Thus by the end of the Ice Age men of our own kind *(Homo sapiens modernis)* had made substantial progress as both physical and spiritual beings. They had developed their manual skills and their ability to work a wide variety of different materials; their hunting methods and equipment had improved, and they had begun the systematic exploitation of food sources. At the same time man had become more aware of the world about him, and indeed of other men, and had learned to communicate his feelings about them not only by actions but in words and in art as well.

In the period immediately following the end of the Ice Age, these important advances led to an increase in populations and to progress towards that most vital of human achievements, the domestication of plants and animals. Progress of this kind was most rapid in a few relatively restricted areas of the Old World—Palestine, Syria, northern Mesopotamia and Iran. These were the areas where wild species of plants and animals that could most easily and valuably be domesticated flourished. They included edible grasses like wheat and barley, and animals like the sheep and the goat.

Archaeologists now know of both caves and open settlements in Palestine and in the Zagros Mountains, on the western fringe of Iran, where people were able to settle permanently by diligently exploiting the local wild animals and plants. At Shanidar in the foothills of the Zagros Mountains, for example, the settlers learned to select young male goats for butchering, thereby preserving the females for breeding, and perhaps for

producing milk and cheese. They also harvested and used wild cereals that grew near their home. The same seems to be true of the inhabitants of settlements like Eynan and Jericho in Palestine. Within little more than a thousand years those peoples and their descendants achieved the domestication of the sheep and the goat, by a continuing process of selective breeding. In the same period they also learned to store grain, and eventually to sow and reap barley and wheat. It is worth remembering that the process of selective breeding still continues today as farmers search for higher yields of livestock and crops to feed the world's ever-increasing population.

For a variety of reasons the domestication of plants and animals resulted in a further growth in population. The rigours of nomadic life were now replaced by an altogether more settled existence, and the dangers and uncertainties of the hunt gave place to a more assured and controlled way of getting food. In such conditions people almost certainly lived longer. At the same time the possibility of growing more crops and rearing more animals, coupled with the temptation to spread the added

burden of work involved, may well have encouraged the growth of larger families.

Even at sites as ancient as those at Shanidar and Eynan, open settlements of circular or oval huts testify to the beginnings of village communities. At Eynan there were perhaps as many as 50 huts in use at any one time. At Jericho developments were even more dramatic. By about 8000 B.C. Jericho was a town of between eight and ten acres, defended by a great ditch and a stone wall with towers, and housing a population estimated at about 2,000 people. The land outside the wall must have been irrigated with water from the spring which makes Jericho almost an oasis in the dry Jordan valley. Clearly the organization of so large a town for defence and irrigation must have involved the emergence of some sort of central authority.

About 8000 B.C. Jericho undoubtedly possessed many of the features we normally associate with the first civilizations of western Asia—a walled town, a large population, communal irrigation, a central authority, and before long at least one temple or shrine. Yet we do not claim that Jericho was civilized. Why? What did the earliest civilizations of the Near East have that Jericho did not? What, in fact, is civilization?

Perhaps there is no single, simple definition of the word that could satisfy everybody. Nevertheless, all the civilizations of the ancient world shared certain characteristics that set them apart from barbarian communities. All of them created societies that were economically and socially complex, and developed the technical and administrative skills with which to make them so. All of them had organized centres of population and ceremony on which to focus both their economic and social activities. In all of them there were people who were freed, or partially freed, from the task of food production and thus able to pursue skilled crafts and even the arts; as a result they all produced material objects—buildings, bronze tools, clay vases or whatever—that

Above: Cave paintings found in northern Spain and southern France, some dating back to 40,000 B.C., testify to Stone Age man's artistic ability as well as to his preoccupation with the animals of the chase. This painting, discovered in the famous cave at Lascaux, France, features stags. Thousands of years later, groups of men still dependent on animals for their livelihood were to follow reindeer migrations, paving the way for the domestication of animals. The antler-masked "sorcerer," left, may well have been a man selected by his fellows to intercede on their behalf with supernatural powers.

Distribution of the cave paintings so far found in western Europe. Many of the most famous are in northern Spain and along the Dordogne river in the Massif Central of southern France.

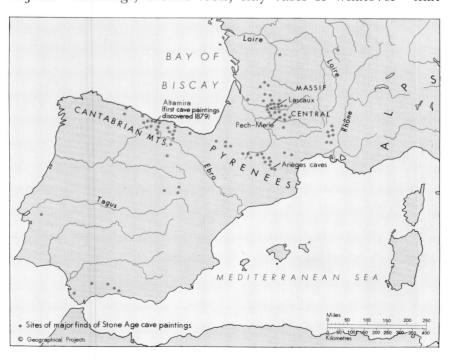

15

were not only serviceable but often beautiful as well. And it is from the surviving remains of these things that the archaeologist can piece together a picture of the past and distinguish a civilized society from a barbarian one.

A complex *economy* is characterized by the division and specialization of labour, by the introduction of standard weights and measures, by public and private warehouses and stores, and by visible exports and imports to and from distant regions. Many technical skills are needed to make these things possible—increasingly advanced building methods for the erection of larger buildings, improvements in transportation, and the ability to work a wide range of animal, vegetable and mineral products, especially a variety of metals. A complex *society* reveals its social distinctions in the different ways in which individuals are treated and equipped, both in life and in death, according to their wealth and status.

Large and complicated communities also need to be ordered and disciplined, and for this they must have laws. Some of the laws governing the activities of ancient civilizations were written down in documents that survive to this day. Writing is, of course, equally valuable for many other purposes, not least for keeping accounts, so that the appearance of a system of writing is also an important feature of civilization.

Social and economic activities of the sort mentioned above can only be successfully developed and integrated when they are brought together in one place. The heart of a civilization—as the Latin root of the word itself implies—must therefore be the town or city. The city is an artificial environment in which man's other, equally artificial, creations can be brought together and fused into a single way of life which we call civilization.

A civilized society, then, is one which has all, or at least most, of the following attributes: Towns or cities, law and an authority to uphold it, developed technology, specialized workers, including artists and craftsmen, social stratification, and a system of writing. It is because the town of Jericho in 8000 B.C. lacked all but the first two of these that we do not regard it as representing a civilized stage of life.

The earliest societies to reveal most or all of the hallmarks of civilization had one outstanding feature in common, their geographical locations. All four of them—the civilizations of Mesopotamia, Egypt, the Indus valley and China—were focused in the flood plain of a great river. These river valleys, with their rich deposits of alluvium and their invaluable supplies of fresh water that could be used to irrigate crops and support animal life, all possessed tremendous food-producing potential. At the same time the geographical uniformity of the landscape in each region encouraged cultural, and in time political, uniformity. Yet this potential for economic and social growth could only be fully realized where men were prepared to cooperate in the equitable use of irrigation water, the cultivation and protection of agricultural land, and the building and organization of settlements to house not only agricultural workers but also those with other skills.

Some of the world's earliest farmers, reaping their crops of grain outside the walls of Jericho around 7000 B.C. The goats and sheep in the background were already domesticated, as a result of a long-continued process of selective breeding. Right: One of the stone towers that defended Jericho's walls.

Progress from a state of barbarism to a state of civilization may be very rapid, as in Egypt, where the crucial developments may have taken place in a few centuries, or it may extend over several thousand years, as it did in the area around Jericho. But however fast or however slow the transition may have been, what happened in the centuries *before* civilization played an important part in determining the character of each civilization when it did emerge. So, too, did the natural environment of the region concerned—its soils, climate, and natural resources.

Geographical setting and cultural history between them ensured that the various civilizations of antiquity were each distinctive and highly individual. Nevertheless they all had much in common, and this should not surprise us. Man, wherever he lives, faces many of the same problems and shares many of the same fears as his fellow men elsewhere. Above all he shares the same great aspiration—to make for himself a better world than that with which nature has provided him.

2 Early Civilization in Mesopotamia

Mesopotamia, which means "between rivers," is the great tract of land that lies between the rivers Euphrates and Tigris. Both rivers rise in the mountains of eastern Asia Minor and flow eventually into the Persian Gulf, the winding Euphrates having a course of 1,750 miles (2,800 kilometres), the more-direct-flowing Tigris a course of some 1,150 miles (1,840 kilometres). Today they merge before reaching the sea, but before history began their whole courses flowed separately. Both offer opportunities for irrigation and navigation, but because the Euphrates floods less violently than the Tigris it is in some respects the more useful of the two. This is particularly true of the river in its southern reaches, where it crosses the broad, flat plains of Babylonia. Here it not only provides the means of irrigating the land but also deposits alluvium to enrich it.

Yet it was not here, where so many circumstances favoured agriculture, that the first farmers of the Near East were to be found. They were to be found instead in the hills and mountains to the east—the Zagros Mountains; to the north in southeast Asia Minor and to the west in Palestine. It was there that edible grasses grew wild, suggesting the possibility of crop raising, and wild sheep and goats grazed, giving the opportunity to domesticate animals. In those areas the first farming communities sprang up by about 7000 B.C. Similar communities spread into northern Mesopotamia by about 6000 B.C. and into the southern part of the region shortly before 5000 B.C.

Once farmers, already equipped with simple ploughs, had settled in the south they were quick to band together to irrigate their land with water from the great rivers. Then the rich soil yielded heavy crops, enabling it to support a large population.

By 4000 B.C. populous towns were developing with mud-brick houses and large temples that were clearly focal points of communities. The temples seem to imply the emergence of a priestly class in the region. Other specialists certainly included potters

Two dignitaries approaching the ziggurat which dominated the city of Ur, about 2100 B.C. This vast structure, rising platform on platform to support a great temple, reached the height of a modern six-storey building. Reed matting reinforced the mud-brick platform construction.

BLACK SEA

CAUCASUS

CASPIAN SEA

Asia Minor

HITTITES

Kizil Irmak

Halys

TAURUS MTS.

Tarsus

CRETE

CYPRUS

MEDITERRANEAN SEA

Ugarit

Byblos

PHOENICIA

Sidon

Tyre

Megiddo

Jericho

Jordan

Dead Sea

LOWER EGYPT

Giza

Heliopolis

Memphis

Libyan

GULF OF SUEZ

Sinai Pena.

GULF OF AQABA

UPPER

Desert

EGYPT

Thebes

TROPIC OF CANCER

ELEPHANTINE I.

Nile

NUBIA

Blue Nile

White Nile

Carchemish

Haran

Euphrates

Tadmor

AMURRU

Mari

Syrian

Damascus

Desert

Murat

Lake Van

Tigris

ASHUR

Mesopotamia

ASSYRIA

Nineveh

Arbela

Ashur

ZAGROS

Lake Sevan

Kura

Araxes (Aras)

Lake Urmia

MEDI

ELBU

KASSITES

AKKAD

Tigris

Sippar

Babylon

Kish

BABYLONIA

Nippur

SUMER

CHALDEA

Uruk

Ur

Susa

MTS.

ELAM

Probable former coastline & river course

PERSIAN

BAHRAIN

Arabian

Penins

RED SEA

Peninsula

GULF OF ADEN

PUNT ?

Direction of penetration of Semitic tribes from the desert, and the mountain tribes from the north east.

Miles
100   200   300   400   500

Kilometres
0 100 200 300 400 500 600 700 800

© Geographical Projects

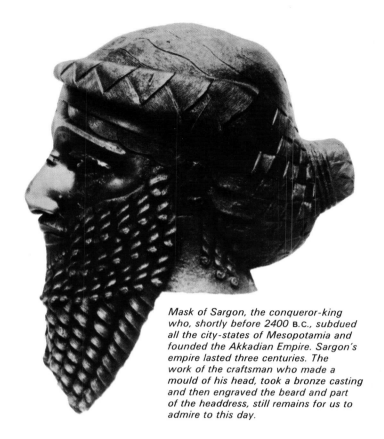

Mask of Sargon, the conqueror-king who, shortly before 2400 B.C., subdued all the city-states of Mesopotamia and founded the Akkadian Empire. Sargon's empire lasted three centuries. The work of the craftsman who made a mould of his head, took a bronze casting and then engraved the beard and part of the headdress, still remains for us to admire to this day.

and probably metalworkers. But metal ores, as well as stone and timber to construct durable buildings, were almost nonexistent in southern Mesopotamia; and the need for them led to the beginnings of trade with regions to both the north and the east. Over the next five centuries, more and more land came under irrigation, more and more specialist crafts came into being, and the volume of commerce steadily grew. All this encouraged the growth of still larger towns and more highly organized communities, and by about 3500 B.C., or shortly afterwards, civilization had emerged in Mesopotamia.

From this time onwards city-states grew up, with considerable rural populations dependent on them. Each city, ruled by a priesthood among whom one man was preeminent, had its own laws and its own god; and each traded both with its neighbours and with regions farther afield. Law, religion and commerce all called for the keeping of records, and thus encouraged the rapid development of a system of writing.

From the beginning, some cities were larger and more prosperous than others, and as time passed a few of them inevitably began to expand the areas they controlled at the expense of others. Shortly before 2400 B.C. a king called Sargon established an empire which eventually stretched from the Persian Gulf northwards to the upper reaches of the Tigris and westwards to the Mediterranean. By 2100 B.C. this had been swept away and replaced by a rather smaller empire, ruled by kings of the Third Dynasty (line of kings) of the ancient city of Ur. A century later this empire also fell—to invaders from the western desert called

Around the Euphrates and Tigris, part of the "Fertile Crescent," settled living quickly flourished. But the early civilizations of Mesopotamia were often under attack from neighbouring desert tribes and raiders from the mountains to the northeast (see arrows).

21

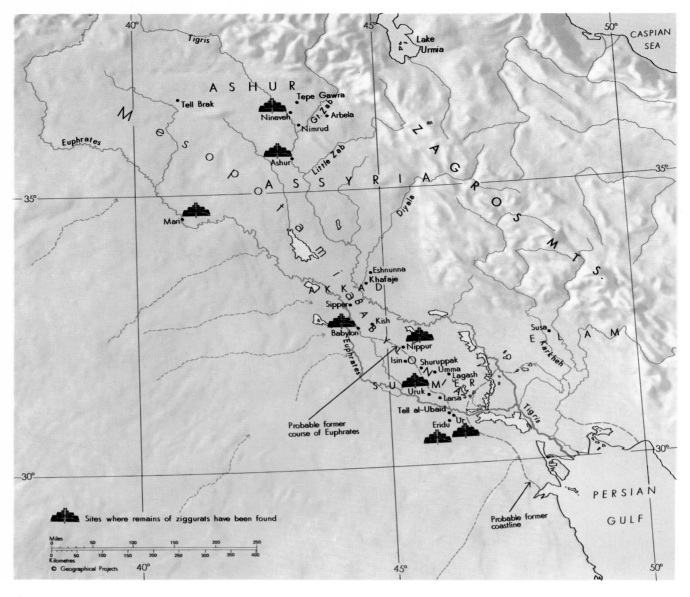

the Amurru (Amorites)—and during the period of chaos that resulted the kingdom of Assyria emerged for the first time as a state of some importance.

Yet although Assyria, in northern Mesopotamia, was later to create one of the great empires of the ancient world (see chapter 7) it was long overshadowed by the growing power of its southern neighbour Babylon, which culminated in the reign of the great king Hammurabi (c. 1790–1750 B.C.). Babylon retained control of much of Mesopotamia until it was eventually attacked and destroyed by the Hittites of Asia Minor in 1595 B.C. Shortly afterwards, when the Hittite army withdrew, Kassite tribesmen from the hills to the northeast of Babylon swept down and established control of the country—a control that was to last for another 500 years.

This brief summary of the history of Mesopotamia—especially southern Mesopotamia—with its emphasis on conquest and invasion, may suggest that it was into warfare that the people of the region put their greatest effort and made the most progress. But this is by no means correct. It is true that by 2500 B.C. the cities of Sumer had armies clad in protective battle clothing, armed with spears, clubs, axes and bows, and equipped with both four-wheeled and two-wheeled war carts; we also know that

The major cities that grew up in the plain of Mesopotamia. The first to be established were those in the south, among them Ur, Eridu and Lagash—each the centre of a small city-state with its own laws and its own god. In time some expanded at the expense of others, and eventually a few, such as Babylon and Nineveh, became the capitals of extensive empires extending far beyond the confines of Mesopotamia.

Although the Sumerians' progress in peaceful arts overshadowed their military interests, they nevertheless armed their soldiers well. Above right is a Sumerian narrow-bladed axe, with its sharp copper head socketed to hold it firmly to the handle. The vehicle shown right, which appears on the Standard of Ur—a Sumerian receptacle ornamented with mosaics—was probably a mobile armoury to drive into battle, or possibly a forerunner of the chariot, soon to be developed.

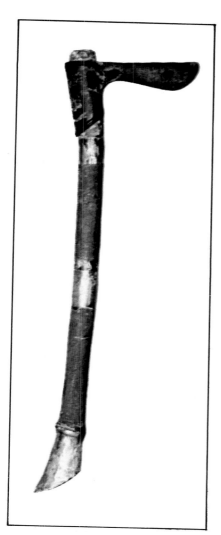

these armies marched in proper ranks and could form a formidable phalanx in battle. But these developments in the art of warfare were completely overshadowed by progress in peaceful pursuits.

Such pursuits were centred on the city, where a brick defence wall, sometimes with projecting bastions, enclosed hundreds of flat-roofed, one-storey mud-brick houses, together with smaller numbers of larger houses and other buildings. Public buildings, in particular, showed considerable advances in constructional techniques, such as the use of columns and buttresses and the building of true arches. By far the largest and most numerous of these public buildings were the temples. In the city of Ur, for example, the whole of the centre of the city was occupied by a great sacred enclosure that contained not only temples but also storehouses, offices, and official residences. Within the sacred enclosure was a second, yet more sacred one, in which stood a *ziggurat*—a kind of step-pyramid made up of four massive rectangular platforms, one upon another. The topmost platform carried the sanctuary of the moon god, where the king of Ur performed sacred rites on behalf of his people.

From the priests who governed each city in its earliest years, a king had emerged as clearly the most powerful figure. He was in fact considered to be the direct representative of the city's god. Beneath him was a large and highly organized body of priests holding many different offices. While some of these offices were connected with religious affairs, many were concerned with administration, law and commerce.

Long-distance trading also developed as civilization came to full flower. Its origin lay in Mesopotamia's need to obtain certain basic materials from abroad, such as stone, metal and timber; but increasing prosperity, the constant need for new and

better weapons, and improving methods of transport stimulated the import of more exotic goods as well. By about 2000 B.C. well-established trading links reached not only to Iran, Asia Minor, Syria and Egypt but also down the Persian Gulf, past Bahrain and Oman, and on to India. Westwards, access to the Mediterranean coasts of Syria and Lebanon may also have led to commercial contacts of some sort with Cyprus and Crete. Written records tell us that, apart from importing the basic raw materials they needed, the Mesopotamian states also sought precious stones, pearls, ivory and even certain kinds of vegetables. Their main exports were grain, wool, oil, clothing, and leather goods. Where possible these goods were transported by river boats or sea-going ships, but elsewhere great overland caravans of up to 200 donkeys were employed. In addition to the rivers, canals also played a great part in intercity trade within southern Mesopotamia. Thus although the wheel—at first a disc made of three parts pegged together—had been invented there before 3000 B.C., carts never became as important as boats and rafts for long-distance transport.

Besides inventing the wheel, the people of Mesopotamia also made several other important technological advances. Before 2000 B.C. they had learned to blend metals to make a variety of hard alloys, to extract silver from lead ores, to cast bronze objects in complex moulds made of up to four different parts, and to produce superb sheet-gold jewellery and ceremonial helmets.

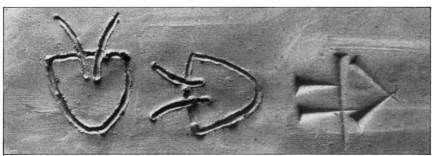

Top: Impression from a Babylonian cylinder seal, bearing owner's name in cuneiform characters. Some 2000 years before this seal was made, the Sumerians had incised simple pictures on seal stones, and from them cuneiform writing had evolved. The diagram above shows how picture of ox head became cuneiform character for "ox." Right: Stele, showing Hammurabi (seated) and part of his code of laws, exemplifying one of the many important uses to which writing was put by about 1800 B.C.

Perhaps the Sumerians' most important invention, however, and the one which did most to advance their civilization, was a system of writing. Before 4000 B.C. they were already using small stones with incised signs or pictures on them to impress designs into soft clay. From the signs on these sealstones there developed a simple type of picture writing which, by about 3200 B.C., was being used to write information on small tablets of clay or occasionally of stone. People soon found that they could speed up the laborious task of drawing the pictures by simplifying them still further. As a result, they evolved a sort of shorthand in which certain patterns of wedge-shaped impressions made with the tip of a writing stick represented certain objects, actions or even, in course of time, certain sounds. This kind of writing, which we call *cuneiform* (from the Greek word for wedge), was adopted by many later peoples in Mesopotamia, even though their languages were different from the Sumerian language originally associated with cuneiform.

It is from the many thousands of cuneiform tablets which archaeologists have unearthed and learned to read that we have discovered so much about the history, religion, science, law and commerce of Mesopotamia. The earliest tablets so far deciphered prove to be ration lists and lists of commodities, but these are soon followed by others dealing with all kinds of topics. Particularly interesting are the many tablets that turn out to be school exercises in grammar, spelling or mathematics. They remind us that a large number of clerks and scribes had to be trained and maintained, simply to organize and record the activities of other specialist workers.

Because commerce played a vital part in Mesopotamian life, mathematics naturally figured prominently in the school curriculum for trainee clerks, and by 3000 B.C. mathematical knowledge was already well advanced. Two systems of numbering were in use, side by side. One was the decimal system, based on multiples of 10 (1, 10, 100 and so on) and the other was the sexagesimal system based on multiples of 60 (1, 60, 3,600 and so on). Strange as the latter system may seem to us, it proved very useful in all kinds of calculations, simply because 60, unlike 10, is divisible by many other numbers.

With the help of these two numeral systems, coupled with tables showing the squares of many numbers, the people of Mesopotamia could happily tackle multiplication and division, fractions and square roots. They also came to grips with various geometrical problems, and with problems involving unknown quantities that would now be solved by way of simple algebra. Mathematicians established a fairly accurate value for π—the relationship between the circumference and diameter of a circle —and knew the substance, though not the proof, of Pythagoras' Theorem. They used their knowledge of mathematics in particular for the design of buildings and for calculating quantities.

Soon after 2000 B.C. Mesopotamian astronomers were systematically observing the heavens, and with their knowledge of mathematics, including that of how to measure angles, they were producing simple star maps.

25

However, relatively few cuneiform documents deal with astronomy. Almost nine out of every ten so far read are concerned in some way or another with accounts, receipts, contracts and other broadly legal matters, for in such highly complex trading communities law was all-important. Yet breaches of the law were not uncommon, and the written records show that the people of ancient Mesopotamia fell prey to the same temptations and committed the same crimes as men do today. Only the punishments differed. Murder, rape, theft, burglary, embezzlement, forgery, kidnapping and bigamy all merited the death penalty. Less serious offences were punished with fines, or in some cases by allowing the "eye-for-an-eye" principle to operate. Imprisonment, as we know it, was simply not practised.

Besides making it possible to keep records of legal cases, writing also allowed governing authorities to set down their laws in permanent form, and build up collections, or codes, of laws. The most famous of these is the Code of Hammurabi. At Susa, some 800 miles (1,280 kilometres) to the east of ancient Babylon, archaeologists have found most of this code inscribed on a large upright stone slab. It includes more than 260 sections covering not only criminal law but also such matters as the legal regulation of professional fees, and of rates of hire for animals, men and equipment. And shortly before the reign of Hammurabi, a king of Eshnunna had issued what amounted to a prices and incomes edict, fixing the prices of basic commodities and the level of certain wages.

Laws regulating the relations between citizen and citizen or between citizens and the state were not the only ones. Other laws set out to regulate the conduct of interstate relations. These sought to cover such matters as foreign trade and traders, what to do with political refugees, how to treat prisoners of war, and so on. Indeed, commerce made foreign relations so important that the profession of diplomacy sprang up as states appointed the equivalents of today's ambassadors and consuls to represent their interests in the lands with which they traded.

Another profession on which the cuneiform tablets throw light is that of medicine. The Code of Hammurabi devotes one section to detailing the fees payable to a surgeon for the performance of certain operations and the penalties he faced if an operation proved unsuccessful. Other documents make it clear that although the medical men of Mesopotamia had no advanced knowledge of either anatomy or physiology, they could diagnose many diseases and ailments by recognizing their symptoms. Having made a diagnosis, the medical man prescribed salves or medicines. Tablets recording the makeup of some of these remedies indicate that while certain ingredients had no more than "magic value" others were probably genuinely curative.

Mesopotamian civilization not only supported, but actually depended on, a great number of specialized workers. In addition to clerks, scribes, teachers, diplomats and doctors, the cuneiform tablets refer to carpenters, bricklayers, masons and potters. These one might expect, but the mention of hairdressers,

This harp, found in the tomb of Queen Pu-abi at Ur, dates to about 2500 B.C. Probably used for ceremonial occasions, it is decorated with shell, red limestone and lapis lazuli. The pins used for tuning the strings are of gold, and the bull's head that ornaments the sounding board is of wood, covered with sheet gold.

jewellers and cooks brings home vividly just how far the process of specialization had gone in ancient Mesopotamia.

In such a society of specialists it is not surprising that some men were able to cultivate the arts, although it seems highly probable that they did so more for the benefit of the god and his priesthood than for the pleasure it brought them. Sculptors, for example, were largely restricted to producing figures of priests, and later of kings. Beautifully made harps clearly show that Mesopotamia was no stranger to musical performances, but these were no doubt mainly of a ritual nature. Certainly the small body of literature that survives—mainly epic and myth—is of a religious character. The most complete example is the Epic of Gilgamesh. This work, like the intricate inlays which decorate a famous harp unearthed at Ur, may have been inspired by religious, rather than purely artistic, motives. Yet, also like the harp, it reveals an inventiveness and an appreciation of beauty that compels us to rank it as a work of art.

We know the Epic of Gilgamesh mainly from the copies of it which were stored in the library of the Assyrian king Assurbanipal, in the seventh century B.C. Yet the epic itself certainly dates back to the period just after 2000 B.C., and it contains at least four separate stories which go back centuries before that, including one about a great deluge rather like Noah's Flood.

This epic thus typifies Mesopotamian civilization as a whole, for the great strengths of that civilization were its concern for the traditions of the past and its ability to learn from, and build on, the achievements of earlier ages.

Sumerian women enjoying a game played on a board like one found at Ur. We know only that each player started with seven gaming pieces.

3
The Civilization of the Nile Valley

The Nile valley is very different indeed from Mesopotamia, and most archaeologists agree that the geographical differences between the two areas do much to explain the remarkable cultural differences between the early civilizations that arose in them. The Nile is far longer than either the Tigris or the Euphrates, flowing for 4,000 miles (6,400 kilometres) from the African interior northwards to the Mediterranean. Yet only the last 600 miles (960 kilometres) of this course, from the First Cataract at Aswan to the sea, form the Nile valley that nurtured Egyptian civilization. For most of this distance, the valley is a fertile ribbon of land, nowhere more than 12 miles (19 kilometres) wide, bounded on either side by steep cliffs, beyond which lies the desert that almost isolates Egypt from the outside world. Only where the delta begins does the fertile land fan out into a great alluvial plain 100 miles (160 kilometres) long and, at its maximum breadth, equally broad. Geographically, therefore, Egypt is divided into two quite distinct regions—South and North, or Upper and Lower Egypt.

The Nile, like the Euphrates, provides the means of irrigation as well as travel, but it yields its waters and its alluvium in far more dramatic fashion. In the early months of the year, the torrential rains of equatorial Africa begin to raise the level of the White Nile, just when the snows are melting on the high mountains of Ethiopia and swelling the Blue Nile. By July the rush of water reaches the narrow Nile valley of Egypt. The river then floods heavily, depositing great quantities of rich soil along its banks. It remains in flood until October, when the water starts to recede. This regular annual inundation—"the Egyptian miracle"—formed the basis on which first farming, then civilization, became established in the land.

As in southern Mesopotamia, farming came relatively late to Egypt. The first farmers appear to have settled in a depression called the Faiyum, to the west of the valley, around 4500 B.C.,

The Nile, whose annual floods brought fertility to Egypt's fields, was also the country's main highway. Well before 3000 B.C. it was busy with large boats propelled by oars and a single sail. By the time the great pyramids of Giza were built, ships developed from the biggest Nile boats were fetching cedarwood by sea from Byblos.

and not long afterwards there were similar settlements in the valley proper. Progress in other activities was at first slow, but between 4000 and 3200 B.C. the pace of development was rapid. During that time the inhabitants of the valley learned to utilize such materials as clay, slate, granite, ivory, copper and gold—often in an extremely skilful manner. Particularly outstanding were the many and widely varied copper tools and stone vessels they made. Like the Mesopotamians of the same period, they had also begun to produce a shiny greenish-blue glaze for pottery which they made from powdered copper ore and talc. Many archaeologists believe they borrowed this idea from Mesopotamia, but some think Mesopotamia may have borrowed it from Egypt. Either way, there were doubtless contacts between the two areas, for by 3200 B.C. Egyptian art and architecture showed clear signs of Mesopotamian influence.

At about the same time, the two separate states of Upper and Lower Egypt seem to have been engaged in a prolonged struggle for supremacy which did not end until around 3000 B.C., when they were unified under a single king—the pharaoh. There is still room for doubt about what part, if any, the people of Mesopotamia played in these events, but one thing is certain: The civilization that emerged in Egypt following its unification was quite different from that established in Mesopotamia a little earlier; and for many centuries it was less given to warfare.

Egyptologists divide the history of the unified land into three main periods—Old Kingdom (c. 2700–2200 B.C.), Middle Kingdom (c. 2050–1800 B.C.) and New Kingdom (c. 1550–1100 B.C.). The pharaohs of the Old Kingdom, who bore the title "Controller of the Nile Flood," were concerned first and foremost with promoting the prosperity of the land. Ultimately responsible for ensuring that the delta marshlands were kept drained, and barrages, retaining dykes and irrigation canals kept constantly in good repair throughout the valley, they had little time for foreign conquest; and with the desert minimizing any threat of invasion except along the short northern strip of coast, they were seldom hard pressed to maintain the security of their frontiers. The Old Kingdom pharaohs eventually lost their authority, leaving the land to be governed by a medley of local rulers for more than a century, but when the pharaohs of the Middle Kingdom reestablished central control they ruled in much the same way as their predecessors.

The Middle Kingdom broke up in a welter of squabbles for the throne, and while the land was thus weakened invaders from western Asia, known to the Egyptians as the Hyksos, seized control. Bitterly hated, they were eventually expelled by about 1550 B.C., when the country's sovereignty was restored under the New Kingdom pharaohs. Then, for perhaps the first time, Egypt became belligerent. The new line of kings undertook many campaigns into Palestine and Syria, first to ensure that there would be no return of the hated invader, but soon in efforts to build an Egyptian empire in Asia. Under Thutmosis III (c. 1500–1445 B.C.) Egyptian forces reached the Euphrates, and although much of the captured territory was lost a century

The map on the right shows the main cities and temple sites of ancient Egypt. Sites in Lower Egypt cluster most thickly just south of the Nile delta; those in Upper Egypt are mostly between Abydos and Syene, at the First Cataract. The fortress at Abu Simbel, near the Second Cataract, long marked the frontier between Egypt and Nubia. The photograph above, of a bend in the Nile at Beni Hassan, reminds one how narrow was Upper Egypt's fertile land. Beyond the river, the ribbon of cultivation and the fringe of palms, the stony desert begins abruptly. The cliffs in the distance mark the edge of the high desert.

Left: The slate palette of King Narmer, carved soon after the unification of Egypt. On this side of the carving the king is seen wearing the White Crown of Upper Egypt. On the opposite side he wears the Red Crown of Lower Egypt. On both sides his name appears in early hieroglyphic characters.

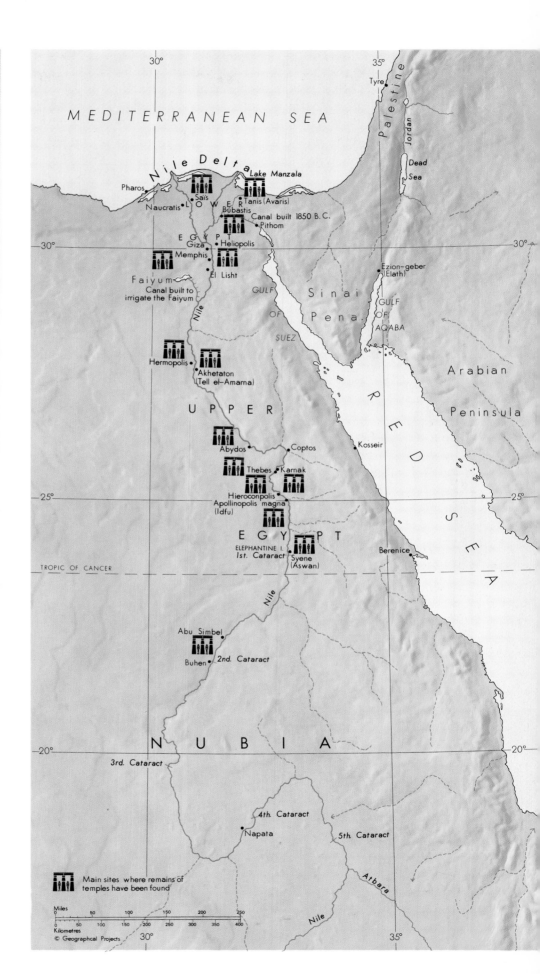

MEDITERRANEAN SEA

Nile Delta

Lake Manzala

Pharos

Tyre

Palestine

Jordan

Dead Sea

Sais

Tanis (Avaris)

Naucratis

LOWER

Bubastis

Canal built 1850 B.C.

EGYPT

Pithom

Giza

Heliopolis

Memphis

Ezion-geber (Elath)

El Lisht

Faiyum

Canal built to irrigate the Faiyum

GULF

Sinai

Nile

OF

Pena.

SUEZ

GULF OF AQABA

Hermopolis

Akhetaton (Tell el-Amarna)

Arabian

Peninsula

UPPER

R E D

Abydos

Coptos

Kosseir

Thebes

Karnak

Hieronpolis

S E A

Apollinopolis magna (Idfu)

EGYPT

ELEPHANTINE I.
1st. Cataract

Berenice

Syene (Aswan)

TROPIC OF CANCER

Nile

Abu Simbel

Buhen

2nd. Cataract

N U B I A

3rd. Cataract

4th. Cataract

Napata

5th. Cataract

Atbara

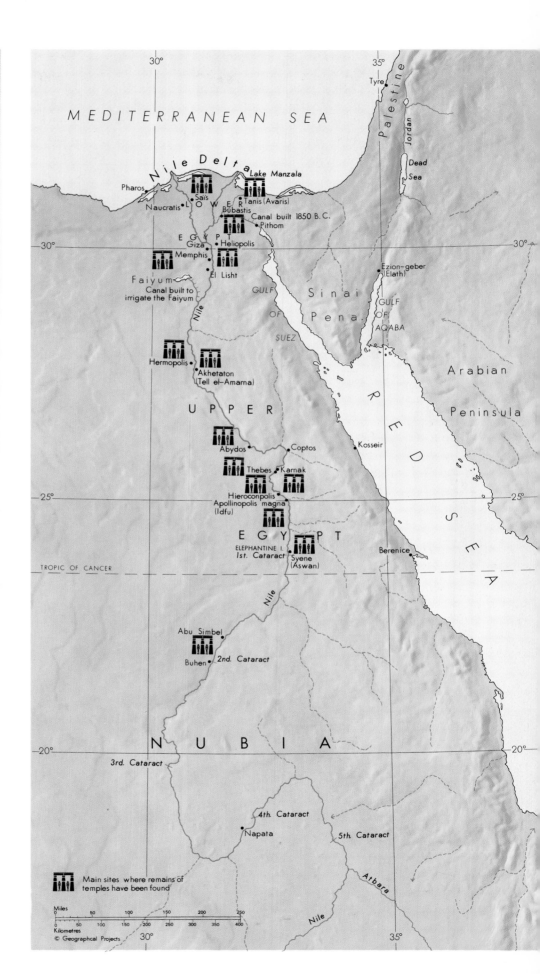 Main sites where remains of temples have been found

Miles
0   50   100   150   200   250

Kilometres
0   50 100 150 200 250 300 350 400

© Geographcal Projects

Nile

31

later, during the reign of the pharaoh Akhenaton, most of the loss was recovered in subsequent reigns. The most famous of the later conquerors was Ramses II (c. 1290–1225 B.C.), builder of the great statue-adorned temple of Abu Simbel. Yet as time passed and weaker kings reigned, Egypt gradually lost its foreign territories, and in due course fell itself into the hands of a succession of invaders—Assyrians, Persians, Greeks and eventually Romans.

Although all these peoples had been in contact with other ancient civilizations before, they were all in turn impressed by the many visible remains of antiquity they met with in Egypt. Two circumstances explain these extensive remains. First, Egypt south of the delta had always had an abundance of stone; second, the work entailed in harnessing the annual Nile floods had long compelled her to maintain a huge organized labour force which, during the actual flood season, could be diverted to work on massive construction programmes. As a result, the great religious buildings of Egypt were of stone, and therefore withstood the ravages of time far better than the mud-brick temples of southern Mesopotamia.

Up to the time of unification, around 3000 B.C., the Egyptians had built in brick and timber. The first great stone constructions we know of in Egypt were the step-pyramid at Sakkara and its associated buildings. Built soon after 2700 B.C., they were the work of a man called Imhotep, whose reputation has survived to our own day. Imhotep's pyramid shows obvious signs of improvization and midstream changes of plan which indicate that his work was in some way experimental—an attempt at something completely new. Yet within 200 years, the three great pyramids of Giza had all been built, and pyramid building had reached a peak never again to be attained.

The pyramids of Giza still stand as a lasting memorial to the incredible industry and technical competence of the ancient Egyptians. The greatest of them, built for the pharaoh Cheops, was made of almost two and a half million blocks of stone, which weighed on average two and a half tons each. Not only did every block have to be quarried, worked, and transported to the site, but also most of them had to be raised to great heights. The topmost blocks were almost 500 feet (152 metres) above the ground. The fact that all this was accomplished in 20 years underlines the Egyptians' staggering capacity for organization.

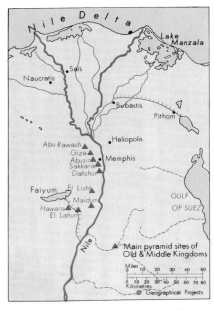

Sites of major pyramids—all on west bank of Nile, south of the delta. The earliest stone pyramid was at Sakkara, the three great pyramids at Giza.

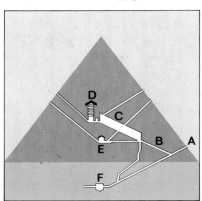

Right: A pyramid nears completion. Every flood season for nearly 20 years, some 100,000 men have toiled at the task—quarrying, shaping and moving over two million stone blocks weighing an average of two and a half tons each. Now only a few of the 4,000 workers permanently employed on the building site remain to haul the stone-laden sledges up earth ramps to the top.

Section of Cheops' pyramid at Giza. F and E are burial chambers which were never completed. The final burial chamber (D), ventilated by two air shafts, was approached through entrance (A), corridor (B) and Grand Gallery (C).

Archaeologists are generally agreed that during the flood season of each of those 20 years, 100,000 men were employed in quarrying and moving stone for Cheops' pyramid. Another 4,000 workers were probably permanently occupied on the site. Pulling the great stones overland on sledges, that ran either on prepared runways or on rollers, required many teams of strong men. Other workers had to cope with the lighter task of pouring water down in front of the moving sledges so that they would run more easily. Where stone was brought from quarries on the east bank of the Nile to the building site near the west bank, as much of it was, even more men had to cooperate in loading it on to rafts and ferrying it across the river. And when the sledges finally reached Giza they and their load of stones needed yet more toiling labourers to haul them up long earth ramps with gradients of between 1 in 12 and 1 in 8.

Although the size and splendour of the pyramids declined steadily after Cheops' reign, other great stone buildings rose in large numbers. Outstanding among these later, mainly New Kingdom, buildings are the temples. Perhaps the most impressive one is the temple of Amun-Ra at Karnak, with its great hall dominated by 24 immense columns, each nearly 70 feet (21.3 metres) high and 12 feet (3.7 metres) in diameter, all elaborately carved and inscribed.

The wealth which made it possible to erect these great buildings and support the kings and priests who used them came not only from the agricultural prosperity of the Nile valley itself but also from trade, warfare and the gifts which generally accompanied diplomacy. The Egyptians traded widely in almost all directions, sometimes directly, sometimes through intermediaries. Southwards, from Nubia, Ethiopia and the land of Punt (probably Somaliland), they obtained gold, ebony, obsidian, ivory, incense and spices, wild animals and dwarves. Eastwards and northwards, to western Asia and Asia Minor, they traded for tin, timber, silver and lapis lazuli, whilst north-westwards from Crete they obtained herbs, beans, painted pottery, woollen goods, and perhaps olive oil and timber.

Many of these goods arrived in Egypt on foreign ships, but others came as deck cargo on Egyptian vessels. Large boats propelled by oars and a single sail were in use on the Nile even before unification, and by the middle of the Old Kingdom Egypt had wooden sea-going ships plying the coastal routes to Lebanon in one direction and Punt in the other. Remarkably, these ships were built on similar lines to the reed boats that sailed the Nile before the first pharaohs ruled. They had no keel or ribs and their wooden planks were literally "sewn" together edge to edge, as we know from the rows of holes drilled along their edges to take some kind of "thread."

Egypt even had a fighting navy of a sort—at its best on the Nile and in the delta, but often relying on ships and men hired from abroad for operations along the coast of Palestine. Nevertheless, a scene of about 1200 B.C. depicts a sea battle between the Egyptians and the "Peoples of the Sea" (the people from the Balkans and the Black Sea area who overran much of the

Giant pillars of the great Hypostyle Hall standing before the Temple of Amun-Ra at Karnak. Built by a succession of pharaohs, the hall was curiously named "Seti I is blessed in the domain of Amun," and described by one of its builders as a place in which the Lord of Gods might rest, and appear in his New Year Festival. Reliefs and inscriptions adorn the pillars.

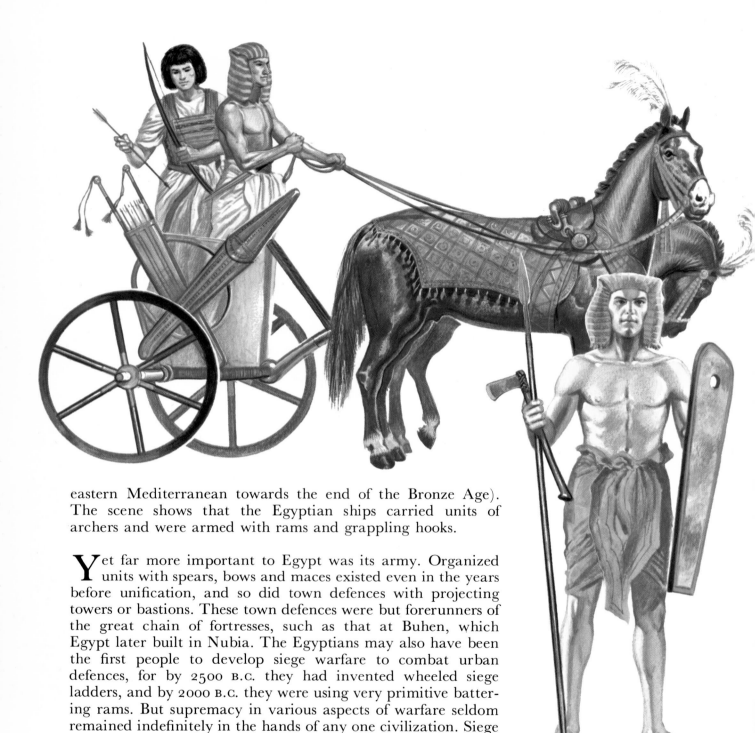

eastern Mediterranean towards the end of the Bronze Age). The scene shows that the Egyptian ships carried units of archers and were armed with rams and grappling hooks.

Yet far more important to Egypt was its army. Organized units with spears, bows and maces existed even in the years before unification, and so did town defences with projecting towers or bastions. These town defences were but forerunners of the great chain of fortresses, such as that at Buhen, which Egypt later built in Nubia. The Egyptians may also have been the first people to develop siege warfare to combat urban defences, for by 2500 B.C. they had invented wheeled siege ladders, and by 2000 B.C. they were using very primitive battering rams. But supremacy in various aspects of warfare seldom remained indefinitely in the hands of any one civilization. Siege warfare later became the particular skill of the Assyrian army. On the other hand, although wheeled war carts were used in Mesopotamia before 3000 B.C. it was the Egyptians who, after about 1500 B.C., made the war chariot a particularly effective weapon.

Chariots played an important part in Egypt's contacts with Mesopotamian and other states which were then continued by a mixture of warfare and diplomacy. The famous letters recovered from Akhenaton's capital, Akhetaton (now known as Tell el-Amarna) reveal very clearly indeed the way in which the great powers of the time were constantly seeking new alliances and political and military advantages. They also record the lavishness of the gifts sent from one monarch to another.

Above: Egyptian charioteers and foot soldier of the New Kingdom period. Chariot-borne archers dashed across the enemy front, wreaking havoc before the infantry lines clashed. The foot soldier relied less on the mace than in earlier times and more on his socketed axe and long spear.
Right: The arrows on this map indicate the warring pressures exerted on Egypt at various stages of its history—from the Nubians, the desert nomads, the Hyksos, the "Peoples of the Sea," the Assyrians, the Persians and the Greeks.

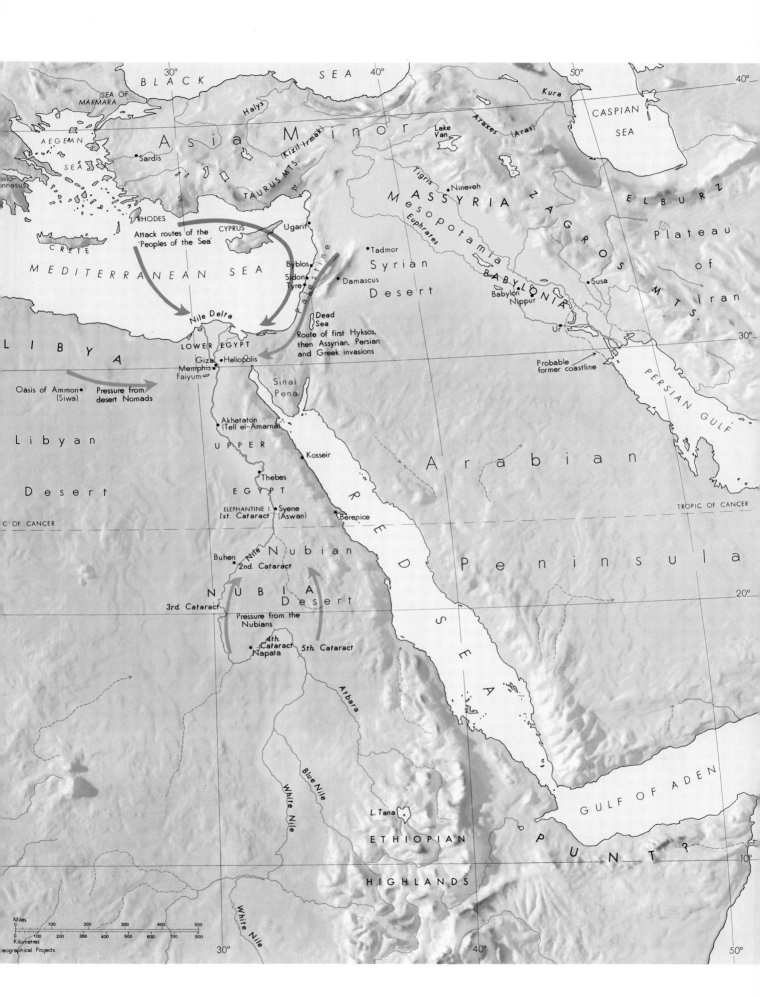

BLACK   SEA
SEA OF
MARMARA
AEGEAN
SEA
•Sardis   Asia Minor   Lake   Kura   CASPIAN
                                                                   Van   Araxes (Aras)   SEA
RHODES   TAURUS MTS.   Tigris
                                              Ugarit   •Nineveh   ELBURZ
                CYPRUS   ASSYRIA   ZAGROS
Attack routes of the   •Tadmor   Mesopotamia   Plateau
'Peoples of the Sea'   Byblos   Syrian   Euphrates   of
CRETE   Sidon •Damascus Desert   BABYLONIA   •Susa   M Iran
        MEDITERRANEAN   SEA   Tyre   Babylon   T
                                                                   Nippur   A   S.
                          Nile Delta   Dead   Ur
LIBYA   Sea   Probable   PERSIAN
              LOWER EGYPT   Route of first Hyksos,   former coastline GULF
                          then Assyrian, Persian
        Memphis• Giza •Heliopolis and Greek invasions
Oasis of Ammon• Faiyum   30°
(Siwa)   Pressure from
          desert Nomads   Sinai
                             Pena.
Libyan   Akhetaton
              (Tell el-Amarna)
Desert   UPPER   Kosseir   A r a b i a n
              •Thebes
         EGYPT
         ELEPHANTINE I. •Syene   TROPIC OF CANCER
         1st. Cataract (Aswan)
C OF CANCER   •Berenice
                 Nile
         Buhen• Nubian   P e n i n s u l a
              2nd. Cataract
                                                                                    20°
      3rd. Cataract NUBIA Desert
              Pressure from
              the Nubians
                4th.
           • Cataract 5th. Cataract
           Napata
                            Atbara
                                                                            GULF OF ADEN
                        Blue Nile
             White Nile   L. Tana
                         ETHIOPIAN   P U N T ?
                         HIGHLANDS   10°
Miles
0 100 200 300 400 500
Kilometres
0 100 200 300 400 500 600 700 800
eographical Projects
                30°   40°   50°

37

The Amarna letters, as they are called, are mainly in foreign languages and written in cuneiform writing, because they are letters sent *to* Egypt. Most of our knowledge of Egyptian history and religion, on the other hand, comes from documents written in hieroglyphics. This remarkable and beautiful form of writing was developed, quite suddenly, in the period immediately before unification. Even in its very early stages, it employed signs to represent not only things but also ideas and sounds as well. The pictorial signs which made up the system were inscribed on clay, ivory, and—most frequently—on stone; but from about 3000 B.C. onwards the Egyptians developed an alternative writing material—papyrus, made from the green stems of the papyrus plant. On this, scribes wrote in various inks, usually red and black but occasionally in other colours, too. Very soon the Egyptians also overcame the difficulty of writing hieroglyphics at speed by developing a cursive ("running-hand") form called *hieratic*. This bore the same relationship to fully drawn hieroglyphic signs as our ordinary longhand bears to our separate "printed" letters. Much later—around 650 B.C.—they invented a sort of shorthand of hieratic which we call *demotic*. All of these scripts were learnt, along with reading and mathematics, in the priestly colleges.

The fact that offending students at these colleges could be given lines as an alternative to a caning is typical of Egypt's imaginative ways of dealing with breaches of law and order. Treason and perjury were punishable by death, theft expiated by restoration of property and a fine, or by beating. Those who evaded taxes were also liable to be beaten, while those who falsified weights or measures might have a hand amputated. Crimi-

Left: Inscription on stone, from the tomb of a New Kingdom pharaoh. Masons were carving inscriptions of this kind in hieroglyphic characters many centuries earlier, even before Upper and Lower Egypt were unified. Soon after, a new writing material—papyrus—came into use, allowing scribes to write at far greater length. Above is part of the Papyrus of Ani, of about 1450 B.C. The entire papyrus contains whole chapters from the Book of the Dead which have been found nowhere else.

Right: Turning the long stems of the papyrus reed into writing material. The stem was first cut into shorter lengths and the rind peeled off. Next, the inner part was finely sliced, and slices were placed to form two layers at right angles on a flat stone, covered with a sheet of soft leather. They were beaten with a mallet until they merged into a single sheet, which was later polished with a smooth stone.

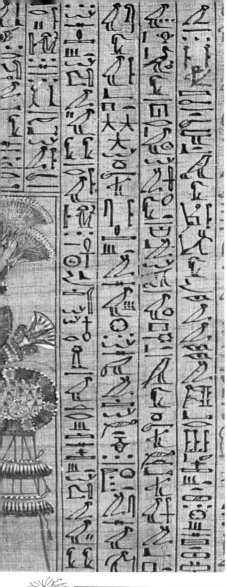

nals could also be sentenced to hard labour in the mines. Trials and lawsuits were heard before local tribunals, or, if they were particularly important, by the vizier. This great man was not only the chief justice but also the chief minister of the pharaoh, wielding extensive powers and having a great number of lesser officials under him.

All these officials would be expected to read and write hieroglyphics, and most would also have a good knowledge of mathematics. Egyptian mathematics were reasonably advanced—in some respects, though not all, more so than those of Mesopotamia. In particular, the Egyptians calculated a more accurate value of π. Mathematicians knew how to calculate the areas of circles, triangles, and rectangles, as well as the volumes of cylinders and pyramids. The accuracy with which they could measure both dimensions and angles is vividly shown in the construction of Cheops' pyramid. Its base is almost exactly 756 feet (230.4 metres) square, the difference between its longest and shortest sides being less than 8 inches (20.3 centimetres). Similarly, its corners are very nearly perfect right angles and the slopes of its four sides are almost identical.

Even more impressive is the way in which the pyramid was laid out so that each of its four sides precisely faced one of the four cardinal points of the compass. Archaeologists believe that the Egyptians achieved this by taking sightings on the Sun, or on the Great Bear. This they may well have done with an astronomical sighting instrument which was invented during the Old Kingdom.

Among the stars that astronomers observed two were of particular importance, the Sun and Sothis (which we know as Sirius, the Dog Star). The former was, of course, at the very heart of Egyptian religion, while the Sun and Sothis together formed the basis of the Egyptian calendar. At some very early stage in their history, the Egyptians noticed that the beginning of the Nile flood coincided with the day when the bright star Sothis rose at dawn. After 365 days the flood returned, and Sothis once more rose *almost* exactly at dawn. They therefore fixed the length of their year at 365 days, dividing it into twelve 30-day months plus five "extra" days.

But because the true year (the time it takes the earth to complete one orbit round the Sun) is nearer to $365\frac{1}{4}$ days than 365 days, Egypt's official calendar got progressively out of step with the seasons—almost one day in four years, almost 25 days in a century. In fact, in 730 years it was half a year out of step, so at the end of the next 730 years it was *in* step once more. Modern astronomers have worked out the dates, 1,460 years apart, when the Egyptian calendar was precisely in step, and because one or two ancient documents refer to times when the dawn rising of Sothis *did* coincide with the beginning of Egypt's official 365-day year, it is possible to date some of the events in Egyptian history quite accurately. The Egyptians themselves became aware of the inaccuracy of their official year and eventually adopted a more accurate one. At the other end of the time scale, the Egyptians were able to measure the passing of the hours by means of sand clocks and water clocks ("hour glasses"), and with the help of devices that gauged the length of shadows cast by the sun.

Though concerned with time, Egypt's people were perhaps even more concerned with eternity. Most of the written records that survive in tombs deal with preparations for the afterlife, and so, too, do the lively pictures which cover the walls and show "typical acts" which would be endlessly repeated in the hereafter. Apart from religious texts of this nature, the Egyptians also produced dramas, short stories, poems and songs. The latter were sung, accompanied by harp and flute. Sometimes, too, harps, flutes, lutes, tambourines and pipes were used to form a small orchestra.

As in Mesopotamia, the harps and lutes demonstrate but one facet of the carpenter's skill. Tomb paintings and sets of tools show us many examples of how carpenters worked and what other things they produced. We have similar information about the production of exquisite stone vases, drilled out with crescent-shaped flint blades, and of copper and bronze objects of considerable size. It was an Egyptian invention—the bellows—that made it possible to melt enough metal at a single operation to cast large items of bronze.

One other craft especially associated with Egypt was mummification. This was practised by a guild whose members were sworn to secrecy about the methods they employed. During the process, which lasted at least 70 days, the brain and intestines were removed and sealed in special jars and the body then dried out in natron, a natural compound of sodium. Then the body had to be washed and anointed before being bandaged. The bandaging involved the incorporation of many magic amulets and written spells to ensure the well-being of the deceased. Although the Egyptians also practised medicine and surgery, as many of their writings testify, it is typical of them that they lavished most care on preparations for the next world.

Clearly the influence of the priesthood and of religion was even more pervasive than in Mesopotamia, for in Egypt it reached beyond the activities of this world to those of the hereafter. Much of a pharaoh's attention and wealth was devoted to preparing for eternity, and the same was true on a lesser scale of the nobles, priests and other retainers who surrounded him. The great temples grew rich on the produce of their estates and the ceaseless flow of gifts, particularly from the pharaoh. By about 1200 B.C. a single temple at Thebes, for example, possessed 90,000 slaves, 500,000 cattle, 400 orchards, 80 ships and 50 workshops.

In terms of sheer material wealth it seems likely that Egypt always outstripped Mesopotamia. The two most outstanding features of Egyptian civilization, however, are the remarkable speed with which it emerged, almost fully formed, in the centuries immediately prior to 3000 B.C., and its equally remarkable conservatism thereafter. The Egyptians soon developed their own distinctive style of civilization, and having done so they stuck by it zealously for the next 3,000 years.

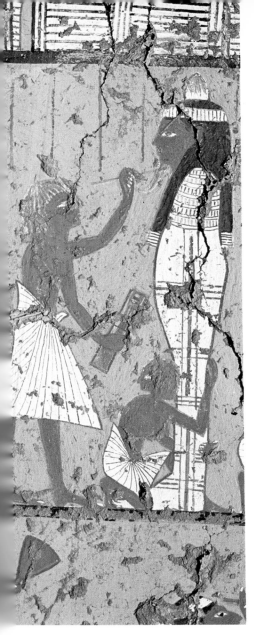

Above: Most of the written records and pictures found in Egyptian tombs deal with preparations for the afterlife. This wall painting, from the tomb of a great sculptor, shows part of the long and skilled process of preparing for burial. Top right: The pendant of this necklace, found in the tomb of Tutankhamen, shows a scarab pushing a ball of dung, representing the sun, before it. This, by convention, symbolized sunrise and resurrection.

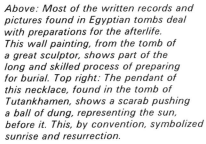

To the Egyptian mind it was of great importance to preserve the bodies of royalty as if for eternity. The diagram on the left shows the stone sarcophagus, containing the three massive, man-shaped coffins, one within another, in which Tutankhamen's mummy was laid to rest. Right: This painted chest, from the same tomb, shows various scenes of war and hunting in which the young king might take part.

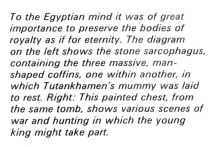

4 The Civilization of the Indus Valley

The narrow confines of the Nile valley provide a marked contrast to the vast plains of Pakistan and northwest India, focused on the valley of the river Indus and its tributaries. Flanked on the northeast by the mountains of the Himalayan range and on the west by those of Afghanistan and Baluchistan, the valley of the Indus covers some 380,000 square miles (98,420,000 hectares). Most of this huge area is now almost treeless rolling plain, but at the time when civilization emerged in Mesopotamia and Egypt it was probably somewhat marshy and overgrown with jungle. Across the landscape roamed rhinoceros, tiger and wolf, as well as the potentially more useful elephant and water buffalo. Added to the dangers from wild animals were those threatened by the great river itself, which sometimes devastated vast areas with its flood waters. But the river also provided fish, renewed the fertility of the soil and served as a line of communication stretching from one end of the plain to the other. The Indus therefore offered man much the same opportunities as did the Euphrates and the Nile.

Precisely how and why it happened no one yet knows, but around 2500 B.C. men apparently seized the opportunities the valley offered and quite suddenly produced a fully developed and widespread civilization. The remains of its settlements are to be found in a great arc around the coast of the Arabian Sea, from the border of Iran eastwards and southwards to modern Bombay, and in a broad area stretching far northwards along the flood plain of the Indus.

Although mystery still shrouds the origins of this civilization, many archaeologists believe it began with a migration of people from the mountainous areas of Iran; and since Iran was in contact with Mesopotamia this might explain some of the similarities between the Indus and Mesopotamian civilizations. Indeed, Sir Mortimer Wheeler, who has conducted many excavations in India and Pakistan, recognizes that the cities of

Street scene in Mohenjo-daro, when the Indus civilization was at its height. An ox-drawn cart passes a bustling narrow lane, as it lumbers along a main street 30 feet (9 metres) wide on its way to the granary. A trader, surrounded by scales, weights and wares, sits patiently while potential customers stand and gossip.

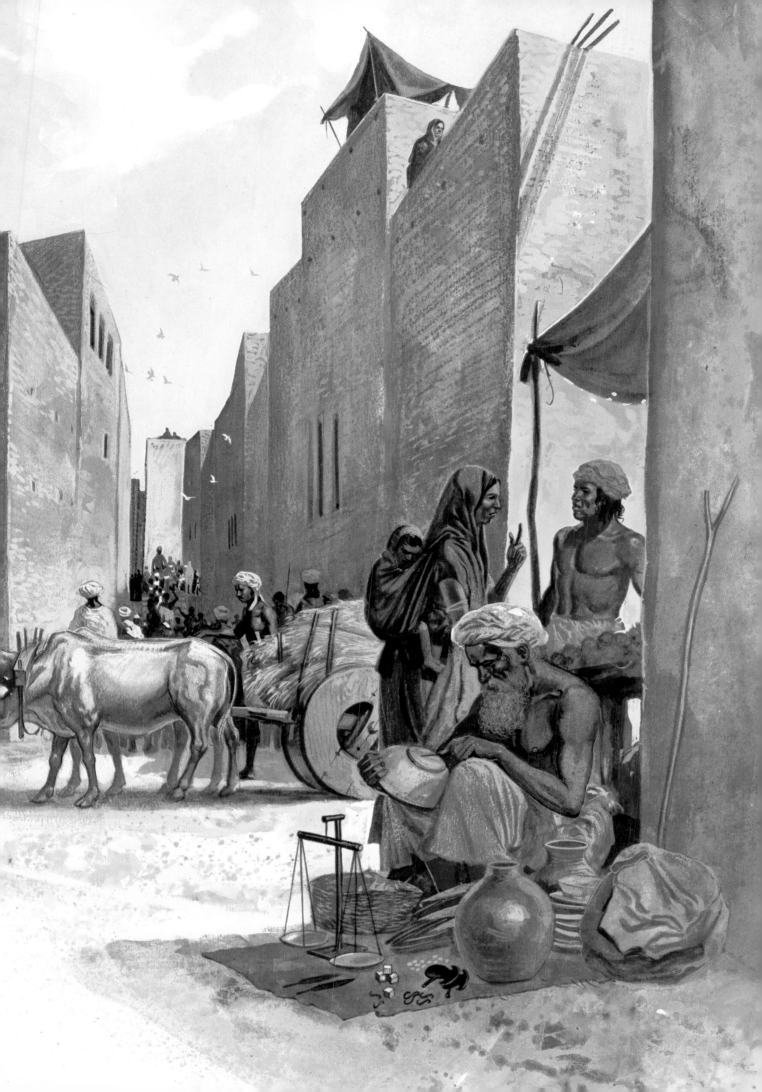

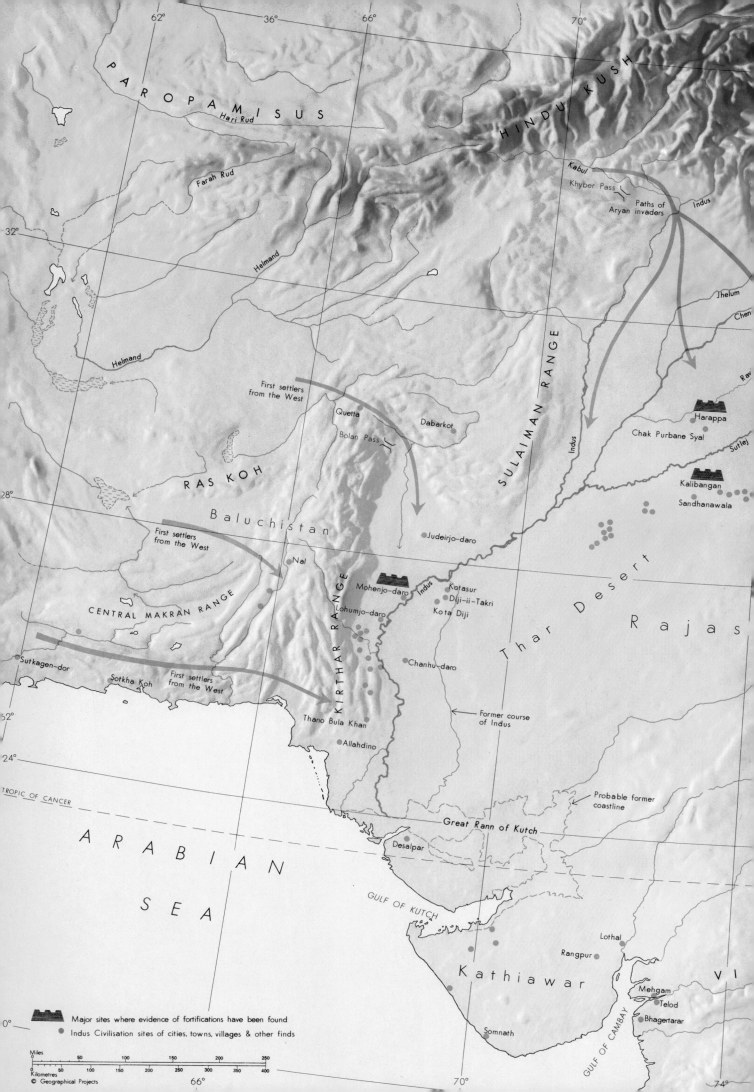

62°   36°   66°   70°

PAROPAMISUS

HINDU KUSH

Hari Rud

Farah Rud   Kabul

Khyber Pass

Paths of
Aryan invaders   Indus

32°

Helmand   Jhelum

Chen

Helmand

First settlers
from the West

Quetta   SULAIMAN RANGE   Rav

Dabarkot   Harappa

Bolan Pass   Chak Purbane Syal

Sutlej

RAS KOH

Kalibangan

28°   Baluchistan   Sandhanawala

First settlers
from the West   Judeirjo-daro   Indus

Nal

Mohenjo-daro   Thar Desert   Rajas

CENTRAL MAKRAN RANGE   Kotasur
Lohumjo-daro   Diji-ii-Takri
Kota Diji

Sutkagen-dor   Chanhu-daro

Sotkha Koh   First settlers
from the West   Former course
of Indus

52°

24°   Thano Bula Khan   KIRTHAR RANGE

Allahdino   Probable former
coastline

TROPIC OF CANCER

Great Rann of Kutch

A R A B I A N   Desalpar

S E A   GULF OF KUTCH

Lothal

Rangpur   VI

Kathiawar   Mehgam
Telod

Bhagertarar

Somnath   GULF OF CAMBAY

0°

Major sites where evidence of fortifications have been found
Indus Civilisation sites of cities, towns, villages & other finds

Miles
50   100   150   200   250
Kilometres
50   100   150   200   250   300   350   400
© Geographical Projects   66°   70°   74°

the Indus civilization were built by people who already understood much about town planning, and believes that these people borrowed the "idea" of civilization from Mesopotamia.

However, recent excavations have revealed something of the settlements and society which preceded the Indus civilization, and which may have formed the basis on which it was able to develop so rapidly. One of these, at Kalibangan, was a fortified settlement with courtyard houses, drains and some buildings of baked brick—far harder and more durable than the sun-dried mud bricks of Mesopotamia. The inhabitants of the settlement knew how to plough fields, and possessed copper tools, wheeled carts and even jewellery.

On the ruins of this settlement, at a later date, a city arose that was clearly the work of the Indus civilization. It possessed all that the older settlement possessed, and incorporated a number of entirely new features, including highly developed town planning. Until Kalibangan was excavated it was thought that probably only two great cities shared control of the whole Indus valley. These were Harappa and Mohenjo-daro, each with a perimeter in excess of three miles (five kilometres). They, like Kalibangan, were laid out to a uniform plan, in which a lower or outer city was built around an inner grid of well-made streets, and this area was overlooked by a well-fortified citadel. Archaeologists have so far found no certain trace of defences around the lower city, either at Harappa or at Mohenjo-daro, but the discovery of a wall around the whole of Kalibangan suggests that the other two cities probably had similar walls.

Within the lower city area the principal streets of the grid system were up to 30 feet (9.15 metres) wide, and each was provided with a brick-built drain. In addition to a drainage system, there were also public wells and probably some sort of refuse-disposal service, for private houses had rubbish chutes that emptied into rectangular bins at the side of the street. The houses themselves varied from small two-room buildings to two-storey structures with many rooms grouped around a courtyard overlooked by a wooden verandah. A block of uniform two-room houses at Harappa has been identified as the home of workers whose job was to grind corn on one of the adjacent circular brick platforms built for the purpose.

Beyond these platforms at Harappa were two rows of six brick-built granaries. A massive granary building was also found at Mohenjo-daro, and it is clear from the size of these structures that vast quantities of grain were produced and stored. Surviving evidence shows that it included both wheat and barley. More unusual crops grown around these cities included melons, sesame and dates. Most important of all, however, may have been cotton, which could be traded overseas. The earliest cotton yet known in the world was found at Mohenjo-daro. At present we have no evidence about the

Major sites of remains of the Indus civilization found to date, including the cities of Harappa, Mohenjo-daro and Kalibangan, each with its well-fortified citadel. The arrows show probable routes by which first settlers arrived from mountainous areas of Iran, and likely routes of Aryan invaders who poured in around 1500 B.C.

methods of agriculture the inhabitants of the Indus cities employed, but, to grow crops on the scale suggested by the granaries, they would certainly have required extensive irrigation works; and the certainty of extensive irrigation, coupled with the size and siting of the granaries, suggests that agriculture was under some form of state control.

All three excavated cities have roughly rectangular citadels, defended by massive burnt-brick walls with offsets and projecting salients or towers. Ceremonial ways lead up through these walls. At Mohenjo-daro the citadel was given over to large, and probably public, buildings. In addition to the granary they included two pillared halls, a large building centred on a cloistered court, and what may have been a swimming pool. This pool, eight feet (2.4 metres) deep, occupied nearly 1,000 square feet (93 square metres) and was lined with bitumen. The excavated portion of the Kalibangan citadel reveals several large brick-built platforms adjacent to many wells and small fire altars.

The size and complexity of the Indus valley cities indicate that they must have been governed by some sort of central authority, and the evidence from the citadels suggests that it may have been a religious authority, like that of Mesopotamia. Yet this is by no means certain, for recognizable cult remains, other than small clay figurines and a few scenes carved on seals, are scarce. The heavily defended citadels might imply a military authority; yet the weapons that survive are simple, and archaeologists have so far failed to find graves of warrior kings. Again, the control of agriculture and the presence of workers' quarters, together with evidence for foreign trade, could be taken to indicate an authority resting on commercial power. But although the Indus valley had a system of writing, excavation there has so far revealed no parallel to the innumerable accounts and contracts of Mesopotamian civilization. In short, the nature of the social organization of the Indus civilization still baffles us.

Much of the mystery surrounding this civilization is due to the fact that unlike Egypt and Mesopotamia it has left no written documents that we can read. A system of writing existed, but it has yet to be deciphered. The script seems to be essentially pictographic (that is, its 250 or so signs are stylized pictures of objects). Single-line inscriptions seem to read from right to left, and those of more than one line from right to left and left to right alternately. But the longest inscriptions yet found amount to no more than 20 or 30 signs, which makes it unlikely that letters, accounts, hymns, laws or myths were ever written down in this mysterious script. It was used mainly on seals, to stamp an impression into wet clay, and sometimes a few characters were scratched on the sides of pots. Most of the inscriptions, therefore, are probably mere labels.

Above: An ox wagon waits in a recess at one end of Mohenjo-daro's granary while its grain sheaves are hoisted up from the unloading platforms.

Yet though we know nothing about the poetry or laws of the ancient Indus valley, we do know a little about its commerce. Many materials, particularly metals, had to be imported,

and we can be fairly sure where some of them came from. The nearest sources of lead, silver and gold were in Afghanistan, and the beautiful blue stone, lapis lazuli, was certainly imported from there. Copper, too, could have come from Afghanistan, but a likelier source—because more easily accessible—was Rajasthan, not far east of the Indus valley. From farther afield came jadeite, found in northern Burma and Tibet, and turquoise, found in Iran. Tin for use in bronze making also probably reached northern India through Iran, although it doubtless originated from farther west.

There is strong evidence, too, for believing that the people of the Indus valley also had trading links with Mesopotamia. First, objects of Mesopotamian type are occasionally unearthed in the Indus valley, and objects of Indus valley type occasionally unearthed in Mesopotamia. Next, from Ur and elsewhere in Mesopotamia, archaeologists have recovered seals similar to those made in the Indus valley and bearing inscriptions in the Indus script. Other seals of the same kind have been found on the island of Bahrain in the Persian Gulf, roughly halfway along the direct sea route between the mouths of the Indus and southern Mesopotamia. Bahrain may well have been an important trading centre, and if so those seals probably belonged to Indus valley merchants who lived and worked there.

The remaining evidence for trade between the Indus valley and Mesopotamia is purely circumstantial. Certain Mesopotamian documents dating back to between 2500 and 2300 B.C. mention trading voyages to places named as Tilmun, Magan and Meluhha, and list some of the commodities obtained there. Archaeologists agree that Tilmun was Bahrain, but are less certain about the other two places. Nevertheless, most of them believe that Magan was Oman, at the entrance to the Persian Gulf, and many, including Sir Mortimer Wheeler, believe that Meluhha was an Indus region port like that at Lothal. The reason for this belief is that the goods obtained from Magan and Meluhha included copper, ivory and wood—all of which could well have been supplied through the Indus valley. However, copper and ivory would soon have been shaped or carved, leaving no positive indication of where they originally came from; timber would gradually have rotted away; and even if cotton, too, reached Mesopotamia from the Indus, it would long ago have vanished. So only indirect evidence remains.

Below: Two Indus seals, carved in stone with chisel and drill, one showing a humped bull, the other a squatting human figure or perhaps a god.

The Mesopotamian documents reveal that trade with Tilmun, Magan and Meluhha was conducted on a barter system, and the same is doubtless true of trade within the Indus valley. But although money was nonexistent a standard system of weights and measures operated throughout the area. Most of the surviving weights are cubes of grey stone. The majority of them are graded in the simple ratios 1, 2, 4, 8, 16, 32, 64. The lightest of these particular weights (1) weighs less than one gram and the heaviest only about 54 grams, or slightly less than two ounces. But there are other, heavier, weights that represent multiples of ten or a hundred of some of these small ones—160, 200, 320 and 640.

Indus pot with painted deer. Some such pots are scratched with characters of the still-undeciphered Indus script.

Indus trade links by sea and land—westwards to Persian Gulf ports and Mesopotamia, eastwards towards Rajasthan, Burma and the Himalayas.

Measures of length were a cubit of about 20½ inches (50.8 centimetres) and a foot of about 13 inches (33 centimetres). These units have been identified by carefully measuring dimensions of buildings and street grids in the principal cities, and these measurements also make it clear that the people of the Indus valley developed a sound knowledge of practical geometry and surveying.

Yet compared to Mesopotamia and Egypt, the civilization of the Indus valley seems technically and scientifically somewhat backward. To some extent this impression may be due to the absence of documentary information, but even where direct comparisons can be made, as in metal working, the Indus valley people clearly lag behind. Although they worked a wide range of metals, including two distinct kinds of bronze, their range of products was strictly limited, consisting mainly of rather primitive weapons and tools. Spearheads, daggers and axes were all produced flat, with none of the strengthening mid ribs found in the Near East, while shaft-hole tools, such as axes, adzes and hammers, were quite unknown. Apart from a famous little bronze figurine of a dancing girl—which may have been made in Baluchistan and not in the Indus valley at all—excavation has revealed nothing to suggest that Indus metalworkers knew of any moulds other than simple flat ones.

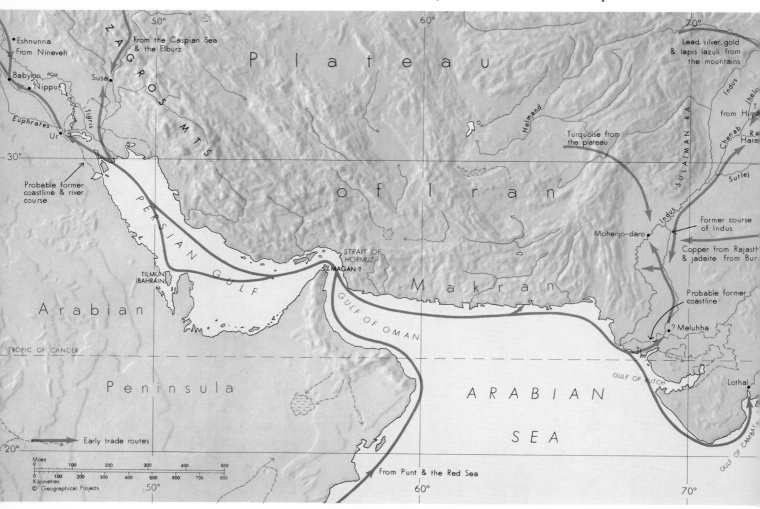

The dancing-girl figurine is thought to show a ritual dance. Many of the seals that have been found are also clearly connected with religion, and, what is more, with a religion that was common to the whole Indus civilization. Perhaps the most interesting aspect of this religion is its apparent link with the Hindu religion that grew up in later times. For example, some seals show a three- or four-faced male god, squatting in the position of a yogi, surrounded by animals. This at once suggests comparison with Shiva, Hindu Lord of the Beasts. One seal shows a deity sitting in the branches of the sacred figtree *(pipal)*, which Hindus still regard as a holy tree; many others depict the humped bull—apparently as sacred then as it still is today.

These and other links with Hinduism are of particular interest because they suggest that when catastrophe brought their civilization to an end, sufficient numbers of the ancient Indus population survived to ensure that at least some parts of their religion would survive too.

The catastrophe came, perhaps, about 1500 B.C., when the major cities and towns of the Indus were overwhelmed by invaders whom we identify as the Aryans. Men, women and children were hacked down and their bodies left where they died. In some places poorly built huts, occupied by people who used a totally different kind of pottery from that of the Indus cities, were built over the ruins of the destroyed settlements.

The invaders, who brought with them new weapons such as shaft-hole axes and short swords, appear to have come from northern Iran or beyond. Almost certainly they may be identified with the warriors of the *Rigveda*, the earliest Indian hymns known to us. These hymns tell of the invasion of northern India by the Aryans, and more specifically of the attacks the invaders made on the fortified cities. One great battle was fought at a place called Hari-Yupiya—possibly Harappa itself.

If it seems surprising that such a vast and apparently well-organized civilization collapsed with apparent ease in the face of attack from less civilized peoples, it must be remembered that Egypt once fell to the Hyksos and Mesopotamia to the Amorites. And in the case of the Indus valley, the collapse of civilization had already begun long before the invaders appeared. From the centuries around 2000 B.C. there is evidence to suggest that people were growing tired of the continuing battle against river floods, and were replacing destroyed buildings by more and more shoddy ones. At the same time deforestation was taking its toll, and Mesopotamian documents indicate that Indus valley overseas trade was declining.

But there may have been a deeper reason for the collapse of Indus civilization. Archaeologists have noted that throughout the whole period it occupied—a period of about 1,000 years—there was little or no change in the material belongings or the way of life of the Indus people. There were no new developments, no new inventions. The Indus civilization, for reasons we do not yet understand, was not simply conservative; it was stagnant. Thus when faced with economic, and eventually military, difficulties, it was inevitably doomed to obliteration.

Indus valley bronze work was normally simple and plain. This dancing-girl statuette, though found near the Indus, may have been made in Baluchistan.

This finely carved head is one of the few stone sculptures yet found in the Indus valley.

49

5 The Civilization of Northern China

When the civilization of the Indus valley was facing the threat of invasion, that of the Great Plain of China was just emerging.

The largest single area of low, flat land in otherwise mainly hilly and mountainous China, the Great Plain stretches from Peking in the north almost to Shanghai. Through it flows the Hwang Ho—the great Yellow river—which now reaches the sea to the north of the Shantung peninsula, but which in times long past reached it some miles to the south. Spread across the plain are deposits of the potentially fertile soil called *loess*, and the fertility of the land is completed by rich deposits of alluvium that the river brings down. Yet the Yellow river, sometimes called "China's sorrow," can be an enemy as well as an ally. All too often it floods uncontrollably and wreaks havoc among the people who inhabit the plain.

Between 4000 and 2000 B.C. the population of the plain was already considerable, and numerous farming villages each housed some 200 to 300 people. Their dwellings were small round or rectangular huts, and they lived by growing millet and keeping goats and pigs. Perhaps about 2000 B.C. new arrivals reached the western part of the plain, as we know from the remains of the new settlements they built, sometimes on sites formerly occupied by the original farmers, and by the new type of pottery they introduced into the area. Similar pottery, made on a fast-spinning potter's wheel, has been found at many earlier sites farther to the northeast, so it seems highly probable that the new arrivals came from northeastern China.

Their coming may well have been significant, because within a few centuries—by about 1600 B.C.—China's civilization emerged for the first time in a wide area on the western fringe

Craftsmen of early Shang China, busy casting intricately shaped bronze vessels in moulds consisting of several parts. Their suddenly acquired skill still astounds us.

of the Great Plain around what is now Honan. What had formerly been a diffuse village-based society using only stone tools rapidly became a coherent city-dominated kingdom with a remarkably elaborate metal industry.

Archaeologists still do not understand how the transformation was brought about. They once thought that the sudden appearance of advanced metallurgy must indicate the arrival of settlers or invaders from somewhere to the west of China, who brought with them techniques they had somehow acquired at second hand from the highly civilized peoples of western Asia. But neither the highly original techniques nor the products of the first Chinese metalworkers support this view. So archaeologists are now coming to believe that metalworking and many other innovations that swept across the Great Plain around 1600 B.C. were due less to outside influence than to the improved social and political organization that resulted when China's first kings—kings of the Shang Dynasty—established their kingdom, which dominated the whole region.

Under the new social order of the Shang kings, agriculture seems to have been organized in a highly efficient manner even though techniques remained primitive. Peasants still dug the fields with stone hoes or spades made from forked branches, and harvested crops with slate sickles, yet the land managed to feed a large and ever-growing population. This was achieved by state control of food production. Labourers were organized in groups under state supervisors, and state storehouses were erected to house their tools. When one of these storehouses was excavated it was found to contain no fewer than 3,500 sickles! Crops were stored in granaries for controlled distribution.

We have no evidence to show that people dug irrigation canals or even watered their crops from wells, and perhaps in the Great Plain, where rainfall was somewhat higher than in the valleys of the Euphrates and the Indus, this was not strictly necessary. But the apparent lack of artificial watering makes it unlikely that the early Shang farmers were able to grow rice. Their ability to feed so many people rested essentially on the regular growing of two successive crops—millet and wheat. They also increased and improved the production of silk, which had begun in Neolithic times. Though no silk fabrics of the period have survived the passage of time, we know of their existence from written documents and from the impressions which they themselves left in the corrosion on bronze objects which were long ago wrapped in them.

The many examples of Shang bronze work that have survived typify the inventiveness that has been the outstanding feature of Chinese civilization throughout the ages. Right from the start, Shang bronze workers produced tools and weapons of singularly advanced design. They included socketed and looped spearheads, socketed axes, elaborate sacrificial knives, a few helmets and large numbers of halberds. The halberds—dagger-like blades mounted like axe-heads on the ends of wooden shafts—were the most common weapons of the Shang infantry.

In the large Shang bronze vessel above food was ritually sacrificed once in ten days to an ancestor named Father Chi.

The bronze wine vessel below, of about the same date as that above but of very different style, was found at Anhui.

Even more calculated to arouse wonder, however, are the intricately shaped and richly decorated bronze vessels. These were cast in moulds that consisted of six or more individual parts, all fitted together with pegs. The bronze cast in these moulds was not always the usual alloy of copper and tin. Sometimes the metalworkers mixed lead as well as tin with the copper, and the proportion of tin or lead or both varied greatly in the various things they produced. The addition of lead reduced the melting point of the mixture. When the mixture was melted in a crucible, there was a risk that some of it might cool and solidify before it could all be poured into the mould. Shang metallurgists overcame this by inventing a heat-retaining crucible with double walls, between which they packed sand and sealed it in. Metalworkers in western Asia never hit on this simple but effective solution to the problem.

The elaborate but carefully chosen decoration of many of the bronze vessels indicates that they were designed to hold ritual offerings of food and drink—perhaps for the ancestors whom men worshipped no less devoutly than their many nature deities. Much of the time of the Shang kings was taken up in one way or another with ritual, and in particular with the ritual that accompanied their efforts to peer into the future. For this purpose the king consulted an augur (soothsayer), and put to him whatever question he wanted answered. The augur then applied a heated bronze point to the bone of an animal (usually a thin shoulder bone), or to a tortoise shell, causing it to develop a number of fine cracks. He next examined the pattern of these cracks and interpreted it as an answer to the king's question. Finally both question and answer were written on the bone or shell, which was then carefully preserved, with many others like it, to form a kind of archive to which the augur could refer at some later date. One such archive, unearthed at An-yang, contained over 17,000 of these oracle bones and oracle shells.

The early civilized people of the Great Plain wrote not only on these oracles but also on silk, bamboo and tablets of wood, as well as making inscriptions on bronzes. Theirs was the earliest known form of Chinese writing, yet their script embodied the same principles as those of the modern Chinese script—that is to say, its 5,000 characters all stood either for things or for actions, and made no attempt to convey sound values. Further, the language of these ancient writings is basically the same as the Chinese that was in use long after men began to keep historical records. As a result, it has been possible for archaeologists to decipher and read the writings of Shang China; and some of them throw light on Shang history and the social organization which may well have been the key to the emergence of civilization in China.

The Shang kingdom was a feudal one, in which rank after rank of the nobility received land, rights and privileges in return for various duties they performed—either for someone of higher rank than themselves or for the king. At the centre of the kingdom stood the king's capital, and the country sur-

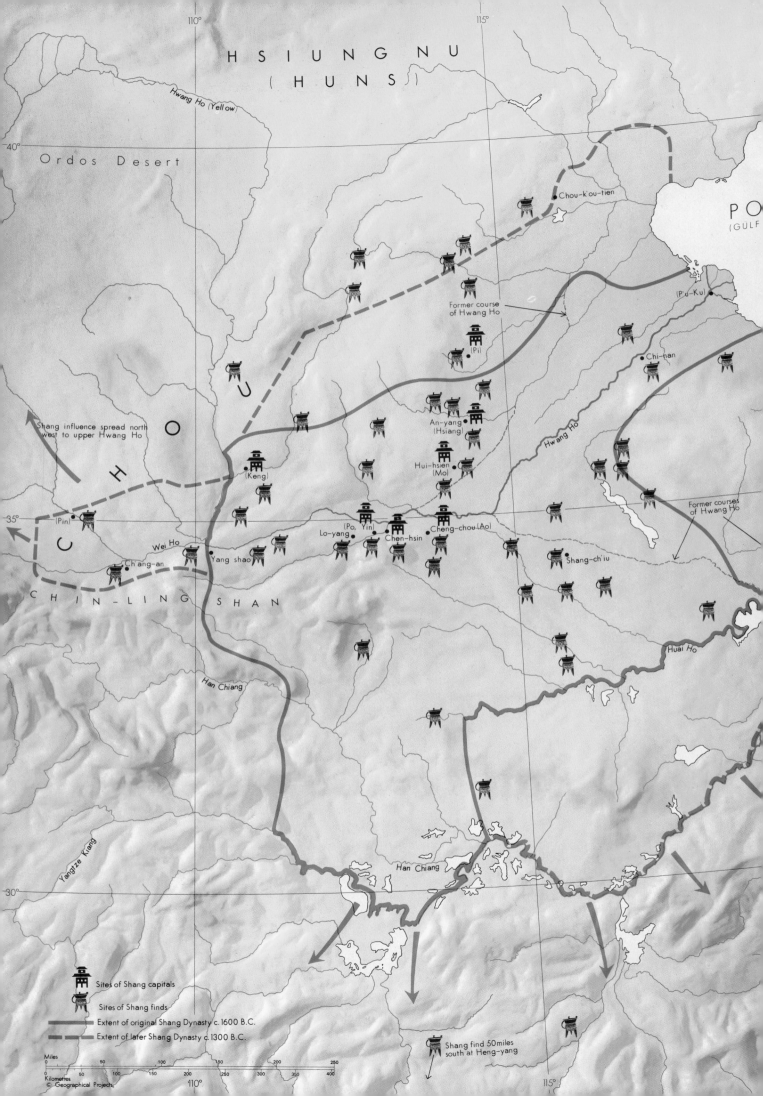

HSIUNG NU
(HUNS)

Hwang Ho (Yellow)

Ordos Desert

40°

• Chou-k'ou-tien

PO
(GULF

(P'u-Ku)

Former course
of Hwang Ho

U

(Pi)

Chi-nan

O

Shang influence spread north
west to upper Hwang Ho

C H

An-yang
(Hsiang)

Hwang Ho

(Keng)

Hui-hsien
(Mo)

Former courses
of Hwang Ho

35°

(Pin)

Lo-yang

(Po, Yin)
Chen-hsin

Cheng-chou (Ao)

C

Wei Ho

Shang-ch'iu

Ch'ang-an

Yang shao

C H I N - L I N G   S H A N

Huai Ho

Han Chiang

Han Chiang

Yangtze Kiang

30°

Shang find 50 miles
south at Heng-yang

Sites of Shang capitals

Sites of Shang finds

Extent of original Shang Dynasty c. 1600 B.C.

Extent of later Shang Dynasty c. 1300 B.C.

Miles
0   50   100   150   200   250
Kilometres
0   50   100   150   200   250   300   350   400
© Geographical Projects.

110°   115°

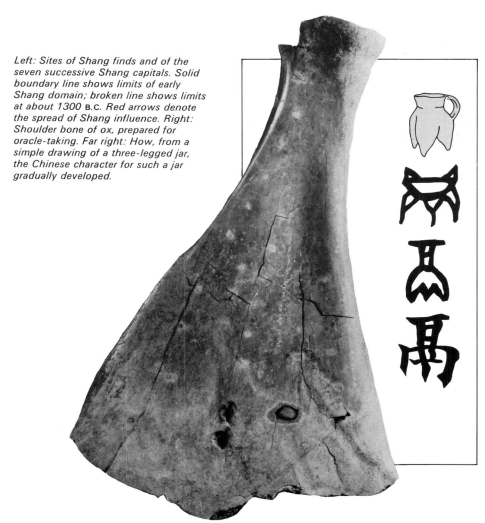

Left: Sites of Shang finds and of the seven successive Shang capitals. Solid boundary line shows limits of early Shang domain; broken line shows limits at about 1300 B.C. Red arrows denote the spread of Shang influence. Right: Shoulder bone of ox, prepared for oracle-taking. Far right: How, from a simple drawing of a three-legged jar, the Chinese character for such a jar gradually developed.

rounding it was divided into four main territories. In each of these were many greater and lesser lords, all ruling their own estates of varying size, and all appointed and protected by the king. In return for the very considerable wealth and power granted to him, each lord was obliged to help guard the frontiers of the kingdom, to raise, supply and provision soldiers in time of war, and to send regular tribute to the king.

The king attended to many of the affairs of state himself, but he also had a great many officials to support and assist him. There were at least 20 different types, some responsible for administering the laws of the land and overseeing agriculture and crafts, others, such as augurs, priests and chroniclers, who fulfilled religious functions, and yet others who had the task of recruiting and commanding troops.

The Shang army normally consisted of three chariot divisions and three infantry divisions. Remains of Shang chariots have been found at several sites, and it is clear that they were drawn by two or occasionally four horses. They had light, spoked wheels with as many as 30 spokes, and carried a crew of three — the driver, an archer and a man armed with a halberd. In battle each chariot was accompanied by a vanguard of 25 men, and a supporting battalion of another 125 troops. Each of these battalions—formidable fighting units in their day—had five officers, 20 N.C.O.'s and 100 privates.

Near the centre of this kingdom, so carefully administered and defended, lay the capital city; but it seldom remained the same city for long at a time. Indeed, during the five centuries that the Shang Dynasty lasted the seat of central government changed no less than six times. The last Shang capital, and the best known, was at An-yang, but the remains of an earlier capital, at Cheng-chou, provide us with most of our present information about the design and the buildings of a Shang city. There an enormous wall, up to 60 feet (18.3 metres) thick at the bottom and made of layer after layer of earth rammed so as to be brick-hard, formed a square enclosure around the ceremonial buildings. Cheng-chou also appears to have started a trend towards the checker-board layout found in later Chinese cities. Nevertheless, neither Cheng-chou nor the later Shang capitals were cities in the sense that we normally understand. All of them comprised clusters of buildings spread over a vast area and separated by open spaces, including fields and cemeteries. Yet together these clusters made up a complex that provided most of the amenities we associate with cities.

One of the curious features about Shang civilization is that it produced no monumental architecture. On the thick foundations of rammed earth found in the ceremonial and palatial areas of the cities, it seems that the large buildings were of humble wattle and daub—a kind of wickerwork heavily plastered over with mud or clay. The small houses that the mass of the population lived in were sometimes of similar construction, often with their floors below ground level, like the Chinese dwellings of the preceding Neolithic age. In addition to palaces, temples and houses, the cities also contained organized workshops where potters, carvers of jade and bone and metalworkers plied their crafts. One workshop, found at Cheng-chou, yielded crucibles, working pits, smelting remains and over 1,000 fragments of moulds for weapons.

Around and beneath the palatial and religious buildings hundreds of ritual burials took place, mostly of sacrificial victims. Excavation has revealed that many of these victims were goats and dogs, but large numbers of men and women were also sacrificed in these areas, and buried either headless or kneeling. Valuable possessions, too, often found their way into graves. Five chariots were found buried under one courtyard alone. Similar finds have been made in royal tombs.

At An-yang archaeologists have unearthed seven great vertical shafts, each approached by four long ramps, and therefore looking rather like inverted step-pyramids. All proved to contain royal burials. The burial chamber, at the centre of each vertical shaft, was built of close-set timbers. Spread around it, and on the ramps, was a rich array of pottery and bronze vessels, weapons, ornaments, carvings of bone, ivory and jade, together with sacrificed animals and people. In addition to common household and farm animals, sacrifices also included monkeys, elephants and horses. A more recently discovered burial at An-yang contained not only a chariot but horses and charioteer as well. Nowhere is the power and wealth

Left: Shang bronze weapons of singularly advanced design: Two arrowheads with spikes to fix into shaft, a socketed spearhead, and a halberd blade eight inches (20 centimetres) long. Above: Two-horse Shang chariot, with its crew of driver, archer and halberdman. The archer's bow, made of various materials bound together, was short but powerful.

of the great Shang kings more effectively displayed than in these royal tombs.

Yet all this wealth and power could not prevent the Shang Dynasty from eventually falling, nor the people of the Great Plain from succumbing to less cultured invaders. Throughout Shang times there were numerous battles against the Chou people of China's western uplands, people who grew progressively more prosperous by raising cattle. In or about 1027 B.C. these people won the last great struggle. The Shang Dynasty was overthrown and a Chou Dynasty set up in its place. But the consequent changes—unlike those in the Indus valley when the Aryans struck—were by no means disastrous. Gradually the conquerors absorbed the culture and way of life of the conquered, and the civilization that had grown up in Shang times continued to flourish.

After more than five centuries of Chou rule, the kingdom broke up into a number of almost independent feudal states, and for a further two centuries these waged constant wars one

Late Shang burial of horses, chariot and charioteer near An-yang. Traces of the wooden shaft remained between the skeletons of the horses, and near their hind legs were the trenches dug to hold the chariot wheels.

When the Chou Dynasty succeeded the Shang, there was no breakdown of civilization in China. This Chou bronze wine bucket, though bearing an intertwining motif never employed by Shang workers, still shows fine craftsmanship.

against another. Then, in the middle of the third century B.C., a strong leader subdued state after state, unified a very large area of north China, and founded the Ch'in Dynasty. It was then that the Great Wall of China, one of the world's most prodigious constructional achievements, was built to safeguard the country's northern frontier. Then, under the Han Dynasties, which spanned the time of Christ, the influence of the civilization that had begun long before in the western part of the Great Plain was extended almost throughout China, and even to other parts of eastern and southern Asia. And although China was later faced with other invasions and further periods of internal strife, its basic cultural unity was by then so firmly established that it has never since been seriously shaken.

The civilization of the Indus failed to endure largely because it was stagnant. That of China endured, and still endures, largely because it has always been inventive. Under the Shang Dynasty, China had been first in the field with multiple-mould bronze casting and heat-retaining crucibles; under the Chou Dynasty it was first to invent efficient breast-strap harnessing for horses, and first to use powerful piston bellows that helped men to *cast* iron tools quickly instead of forging them laboriously. The list of later Chinese "firsts," which includes blockprinting and gunpowder, is equally impressive, and there is no reason to believe that it will not grow longer in times to come.

Map showing the extent of territories governed by the three dynasties which in turn followed the Shang: Western Chou, Eastern Chou and Ch'in. The Ch'in emperors ruled from the Great Wall they built in the north to the Yangtze Kiang in the south.

Gobi Desert

H S I U N G N U
(H U N S)

NAN SHAN

Ordos Desert

Yun-chung

built c. 300 B.C.

built 353 B.C.

Hwang Ho

T'ai-yüan

built c. 300 B.C.

Lung-hsi

Hwang Ho

An-yang

Hwang Ho (Yellow)

Former courses of
the Hwang Ho

PO HAI
(GULF OF CHIHLI)

Shantung
Peninsula

KOREA
BAY

built c. 290 B.C.

Liao Ho

YELLOW
SEA

Wei Ho

HSIEN-YANG
(Capital Western Chou)

LO-YANG
(Capital Eastern Chou)

Cheng-chou

CHIN-LING SHAN

CHIUNG HSIA SHAN

Han-chung

Nan-yang

Shu
(Ch'eng-tu)

Pa

Nan

Yangtze Kiang

Wu

Ch'ang-sha

WUYI SHAN

N
A
N
L
I
N
G

Kuei-lin

extent before 211 B.C.

Ta-lung Chiang

Yangtze Kiang

Hsiang

Hsi Chiang

Nan-hai

FORMOSA STRAIT

TROPIC OF CANCER

FORMOSA
(TAIWAN)

OF CANCER

Song Ca (Red)

Song Bo (Black)

HAINAN

SOUTH CHINA SEA

LUZON

Boundary of Western Chou 1027-771 B.C.

Boundary of Eastern Chou:
a) Spring & Autumn Period 770-475 B.C.
b) Warring States Period 475-221 B.C.
(Where they do not coincide with Western Chou or Ch'in)

Maximum extent of Ch'in Dynasty 221-207. B.C.

Great Wall of China

6 Maritime Civilizations of the Mediterranean

Fashionably attired ladies, their hair elaborately styled, wait by an entrance of the Palace of Knossos to watch as a ceremonial procession passes.

China's civilization, like those of Mesopotamia, Egypt and the Indus, was founded in a more or less uniform low-lying region dominated by a great river which served, among other things, as a highway. Minoan Crete laid the foundations of Greek and European civilization against a sharply contrasting geographical background. Crete is a small and very mountainous island, only 150 miles (240 kilometres) long and nowhere much more than 30 miles (48 kilometres) wide. Most of its low-lying land is found in scattered patches along the north coast, and because of the cliffs that isolate one patch from another communication between them is, in a good many cases, easier by sea than by land.

The Neolithic population of Crete was relatively small, but shortly after 3000 B.C. metalworking was introduced and there was a marked rise in the number of settlements, probably indicating a growth of population. Archaeologists are still uncertain whether or not these changes were brought about by the arrival of new settlers from western Asia Minor. What is certain is that from this time on there was steady progress towards civilization, which showed itself in such ways as the making of fine stone vases, gold jewellery and bronze tools, the building of larger houses and settlements, and increasing overseas contacts.

Shortly before 2000 B.C. a building of palatial proportions was erected at Knossos in the north of the island, and this was followed by the building of further palaces at Phaestos and Mallia, and later at Zakro and other centres. The Minoan civilization, named after a legendary king of Crete called Minos, is considered to date from this time. Although the palaces were seriously damaged by earthquake about 1700 B.C. they were soon restored; and evidence from Egypt suggests that in the period from 1700 to 1450 B.C. the civilization of Crete ranked with those of the Nile valley and Mesopotamia.

20°   22°   24°   26°

Maritsa

42°

Lake
Ochrida
Lake
Prespa

RHODOPE MTS.

THRA

40°

THASOS

Maritsa

Chalcidice

MT. OLYMPUS

IMBROS

HELLESPO
DARDANELL

Troy

LEMNOS

LESBOS

Tricca

THESSALY

Ithome

Pherae

Peneus

Iolcus

Thebes

Pteleum

Oreus

NORTHERN

SPORADES

PEPARETHUS

A E G E A N

S E A

SKYROS

KHIOS

Heraclea

EUBOEA

Mycenaeans cross
the Aegean c.120 B.C.

CEPHALONIA

ITHACA

LEUKAS

Achelous

Thermum

Pleuron

Orchomenus Copais

PARNASSUS

Thebes

ANDROS

SAMO

38°

Aegium

ACHAEA

GULF OF CORINTH

Styra

Athens

KEA

TENOS

CARIA

ZACYNTHOS

Sicyon

Corinth

Philius Cleonae

Megara

SALAMIS

AEGINA

KYTHNOS

SYROS

DELOS

C-YCLADES

NAXOS

DODECA

ELIS

ARCADIA

MYCENAE

Mantinea   Argos

Tiryns

Peloponnesus

Megalopolis   Tegea

GULF OF ARGOS

SERIPHOS

PAROS

IONIAN

Sparta

MESSENIA

Amyclae

LACONIA
(SPARTA)

SIPHNOS

AMORGOS

S E A

Pylos

MELOS

THERASIA THERA

KYTHERA

Minoans trade with
the mainland

36°

Mycenaeans capture
Knossos late in the
15th. century B.C.

SEA OF CRETE

Migration of some
Minoans to Asia Minor

M E D I T E R R A N E A N

S E A

C R E T E

Knossos   Mallia

Zakro

Phaestos

Minoan trade route
to Malta & Sicily

Minoan trade routes to Egypt

🏛 Major Bronze Age settlements

✪ Places where indications of Minoan settlement have been found

Miles
0 10 20 30 40 50 60 70 80 90 100

0 10 20 30 40 50 60 70 80 90 100 110 120 130 140 150 160
Kilometres

20°   22°   24°   26°

© Geographical Projects

BLACK

SEA

42°

BOSPHORUS

SEA OF MARMARA

40°

A C I A

A

s

i

a

H I T T I T E S

Gediz

M

i

n

o

r

38°

Buyut Menderes

Milerus (Possibly founded
by the Minoans)

Os

Ialysus

RHODES
Lindos

36°

KARPATHOS   Mycenaeans settle in Rhodes,
south west Asia Minor & Cyprus
in the 14th.–12th. centuries B.C.

trade route to
Mediterranean

28°

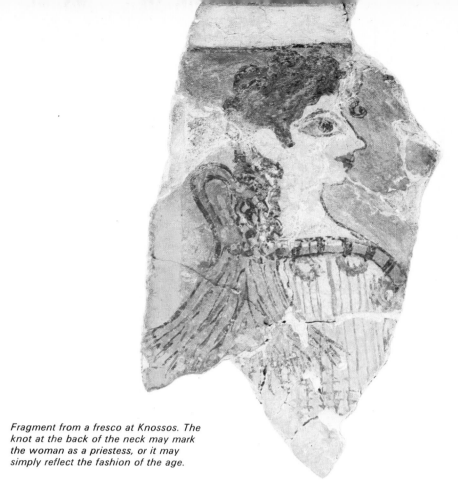

Fragment from a fresco at Knossos. The knot at the back of the neck may mark the woman as a priestess, or it may simply reflect the fashion of the age.

This period of prosperity was brought to an end by a volcanic explosion of a magnitude unparalleled in human history, before or since. It completely blew up the island of Thera, 80 miles (128 kilometres) north of Crete, and the high waters which hit the Cretan coast, coupled with the thick blanket of volcanic ash which must have settled over the eastern half of the island, proved disastrous. From that time decline set in, and within a few decades Crete appears to have fallen to invasion by the Mycenaeans of mainland Greece. The warrior graves of this period found at Knossos are not Minoan in character but Mycenaean; and it was presumably the Mycenaeans who spoke and wrote an early form of Greek preserved on tablets inscribed in the "Linear B" script—the last of the three scripts employed in ancient Crete.

Knossos is the largest of the Minoan palaces, all of which share a common layout and reveal the same architectural features. The Minoans did not build an outer wall first and then fit rooms and courts into it. Instead they began by laying out a great courtyard and then erected the entire building around it. Flanking the central courtyard were storerooms, workshops, offices and kitchens, and over them were built private apartments and dining halls. Beyond the building, on the west side, was a further large court, apparently used for dancing and perhaps communal gatherings.

The palaces, unfortified, were clearly built not for defence but as colourful and pleasant places in which to live. The walls were covered with superb frescoes, often depicting landscapes, flowers

Major Bronze Age settlements of Minoan and Mycenaean civilizations. Stars denote sites of Minoan settlements outside Crete. Broken arrows show Minoan trade routes. Solid arrows show later Mycenaean expansion into Asia Minor, Crete and Cyprus.

63

or animals, but sometimes showing the occupants of the palaces themselves. No rooms, even the inside rooms in the basement areas, were left without daylight, for the builders made frequent use of light wells—open shafts running from top to bottom of the building to let in the sunshine. Floors were paved with gypsum, and below the palace ran a system of drains and clay waterpipes.

Who were the people who lived in such splendour? To judge from the frescoes we can perhaps best think of them as the king, his family, and many courtiers—presumably officials and advisers. But in fact we have no certain knowledge of how Crete was ruled. Greek tradition speaks of King Minos, ruling from Knossos; but Crete had six or seven palatial centres, and may therefore have been divided into six or seven independent states or kingdoms, comparable in size to the later Greek city-states. Yet the Minoan palaces were clearly not the centres of Greek-type democracies. Their concentration of storage facilities, workshops and offices suggests that they controlled the production and distribution of food and manufactured goods, and that wealth and power were concentrated in the hands of a select few.

The same is also implied by the written documents found in the palaces. The later "Linear B" tablets, doubtless written by Mycenaeans, might possibly suggest that the system of control from the palaces was introduced by the invaders. But there are other tablets written in "Linear A"—a native Cretan script—and these, too, are mainly accounts of one sort or another.

The origins of the "Linear A" script are uncertain, but we do know that it was not Crete's first form of writing. Before it came into use the Minoans used a hieroglyphic script, and earlier still they made use of seals to press stylized designs into wet clay. Since these seals were carefully stored, they too may well have carried information.

Some of the later documents, referring to supplies of foodstuffs, suggest that Crete may have been the first Mediterranean civili-

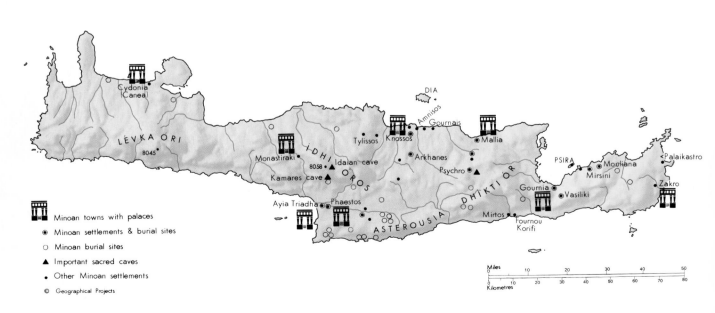

- 🏛 Minoan towns with palaces
- ◉ Minoan settlements & burial sites
- ○ Minoan burial sites
- ▲ Important sacred caves
- • Other Minoan settlements
- © Geographical Projects

Top left: Part of the west magazine of the Palace of Knossos, with some of its man-high storage jars still there. Above: The bull game, in which a young athlete grasped a bull's horns and then somersaulted over its back. Shown on Minoan frescoes and on seal stones, this was a sport in which few modern athletes would care to indulge, no matter how vigilant the companions waiting to steady their landing.

Left: Palace towns, settlements, burial sites and sacred caves of Minoan Crete. Known sites are concentrated in the eastern two-thirds of the island. The forests of western Crete were exploited for Crete's shipbuilding industry.

zation to raise the growing of grapes and olives to major economic importance. Indeed, wine and olive oil were probably among the main exports of Minoan Crete, for Crete engaged in overseas trade on a large scale. She set up colonies on many of the Aegean islands, and at least one on the mainland of Asia Minor, but her trading interests also spread well beyond the Aegean. While archaeologists still argue as to whether or not Crete traded with the western Mediterranean, all agree that she traded with Egypt, Cyprus (an important source of metal ores) and the east Mediterranean mainland. In all these regions archaeologists have found typical examples of Minoan pottery, and in Crete they have found typical imports from all three regions.

The Minoan pottery found on foreign sites is not difficult to recognize, for it is quite unlike anything being produced at the same time in the Near East. Gaily painted in a free-flowing style, and often using motifs drawn from nature, it reveals the same spirit of freedom and enjoyment on the part of the artists who made it as do the Minoan frescoes. Enjoyment also shines through the scenes of ordinary life that artists occasionally chose to depict: wrestlers at grips, boxers and acrobats in action, revellers laughing, singing and music making in gay procession. It is surely also

significant that archaeologists have unearthed no evidence to indicate that Crete possessed a highly organized army, or that its towns were defended by walls and towers. Peace and the pursuit of pleasure seem to have been the principles on which Minoan civilization operated; and if that is true it was clearly very different from any of the four great river valley civilizations.

Why this was so is not easy to explain, but it may have had much to do with Crete's geographical position. Encircled by the sea, Crete for many centuries had little to fear from external enemies; and straddling the sea routes which linked both Africa and Asia to Europe she could reap all the prosperity to be gained from early intercontinental trading. By virtue of this position Crete certainly played a leading role in the transmission of ideas between Europe and the Near East.

For a short time after the collapse of Minoan civilization this role was taken over by the Mycenaeans of the Greek mainland, who traded with both the eastern and western Mediterranean. But around 1200 B.C. they, too, fell before barbarian invaders who swept into Greece from the north. A century or so

Scene in a Phoenician port, about 1000 B.C. A master shipwright works with his adze on a cedar beam, shaping it into part of a ship's keel, while labourers busy themselves with unskilled tasks. Port workers stack up wine jars ready for export, while idlers by the city wall watch a vessel put to sea.

Right: With their homeland a mere 180-mile (289-kilometre) coastal strip hemmed in by the mountains of Lebanon, the Phoenicians inevitably looked seawards for their livelihood. All their important towns were ports.

Principal Phoenician towns

of relative isolation and dislocation of trade followed. Then a new era of Mediterranean commerce opened, spearheaded by the cities of Phoenicia.

The name Phoenicia described that part of the coastal plain from midway between Jaffa and Haifa in modern Israel roughly to Tartus in Syria. Nowhere along this 200-mile (320-kilometre) stretch does the plain extend more than 15 miles (24 kilometres) inland, and in most places it is far narrower. Behind the plain rise mountains which at that time were covered with valuable cedar forests, while along the coast are many small offshore islands and possible sites for harbours.

Even before 3000 B.C. this was an important area for trade, for it was here that the Egyptians bought the timber for building they could not grow in their own land, and that trade routes from the cities of the Tigris and Euphrates and the lands of the Mediterranean met. Soon Byblos became one of the richest cities in the Near East. For much of the Bronze Age (from 2000 to 1200 B.C.) it was rivalled by another city some 50 miles (80 kilometres) north of the area that later became known as Phoenicia—Ugarit. At this time the culture of the people of the coastal strip

67

was basically the same as that of those who lived farther inland in Palestine and Syria—the Canaanites. In the period of invasions and migrations at the end of the Bronze Age the greater part of the area fell into the hands of newcomers, including Philistines and Israelites. The coastal strip, however, remained largely in the hands of the indigenous population, and here there emerged a civilization of city-states—the civilization of Phoenicia.

The Phoenicians were not, in the main, great inventors but they excelled as master craftsmen. King Solomon, builder of Jerusalem's first temple, employed not only Phoenician stone-masons but also Phoenician shipbuilders, and later kings of Israel used Phoenician furniture widely in their palaces. Much of this furniture was elaborately decorated with applied ivory carvings, a Phoenician speciality. The ivories reveal the secret of Phoenicia's commercial success, for they utilized a variety of motifs taken from surrounding civilizations and interwoven into an attractive, even if thoroughly muddled, repertoire. In the ivories, as in all Phoenician products, the workmanship was always excellent; and the range of products offered was extensive. The formula of borrowing and mixing motifs was also applied to the Phoenician silver bowls to which Homer pays tribute. On one such bowl Assyrian, Greek, Egyptian and Syrian figures were freely intermixed in a scene which made commercial sense but historical nonsense.

Other profitable Phoenician industries produced glass vessels, amulets and beads, wooden furniture and, of course, the famous

The ivory carvings of Phoenicia were known and admired throughout much of the ancient world. The one above, showing the goddess of love in the form of a woman gazing from a window, found its way to Assyria. It formed part of a panel on a couch. That on the right, showing a Negro boy being savaged by a lion, also reached Assyria—probably as loot.

dyed cloth. The purple dye for this cloth was produced from the shellfish *Murex trunculus*, and on the sites of the two principal Phoenician cities, Tyre and Sidon, great mounds of these shells still testify to the production of purple cloth.

All these goods were produced more for export than for home consumption. Many were traded to Egypt, Assyria and Babylonia by overland routes, but others were sent westwards to Cyprus, Greece, North Africa and Italy, and these had to be transported by ship. In return for its exports Phoenicia had to import much of the food that its own territory was too small to grow in sufficient quantity, as well as such commodities as cotton, flax, ivory, metals and semiprecious stones; and many of these imports came from overseas. This dependence on seaborne trade, coupled with the proximity of powerful and often warlike neighbours, ensured that the Phoenicians paid much attention to shipbuilding, shipping, and harbour works—so much so that they became the sea carriers for much of the known world, spreading ideas, as well as trading cargoes, wherever they went.

All the known major cities of Phoenicia were built on promontories jutting out from the mainland coast, or on offshore islands. They seem to have been densely packed with multi-storey buildings, but their focal points were their harbours—usually two of them—created by supplementing natural features with man-made harbour works. But the Phoenicians were great colonists, and the most elaborate of their harbours to survive are not found in Phoenicia at all, but in Phoenician cities built far to the west, at Carthage on the coast of North Africa and at Motya in Sicily. Here, in addition to the harbours proper, there are also finely built wet docks, called *cothons*.

Among other valuable Phoenician exports were glass vessels. This scent bottle, in the shape of a wine vessel, was found at Amathus, in Cyprus.

Carthage and Motya are only two of many Phoenician overseas colonies. The earliest such colonies were probably those on Cyprus, but according to tradition a colony was founded on the island of Rhodes about 1190 B.C.—at about the time of the Trojan War. Soon colonies were founded on several of the more distant islands of the Aegean, including Crete, but these were by no means at the fringe of the Phoenician commercial empire. In the western Mediterranean all the principal islands—Malta, Sicily, Sardinia, Corsica and the Balearic Islands—saw the setting up of Phoenician colonies. Others were situated on the coast of Spain and along the shores of North Africa. We still do not know for sure when these distant colonies came into existence, but tradition points to a very early period in Phoenician history. For example, Cádiz, beyond the Strait of Gibraltar, is said to have been founded in 1110 B.C.

The Phoenicians also planted colonies on the Atlantic seaboard—at Tangier, Lixus and Mogador, on the northwest coast of Africa. We know of no colonies farther afield than this, but we do know that after the seventh century B.C., when the power of Phoenicia's homeland cities fell into sharp decline, Phoenician ships operating from increasingly powerful colonies such as Carthage were still making great voyages of exploration. The earliest of these to find its way into any kind of account is said to have begun about 600 B.C. The Greek traveller and historian

Herodotus, writing more than a century later, tells us disbelievingly that the seamen who took part in it claimed to have circumnavigated Africa, taking three years to accomplish that feat. Their accounts of the strange constellations they saw in the night skies and the strange animals they encountered, which made Herodotus doubt the story, are the very things that make most modern scholars believe it.

We also know of two other remarkable expeditions, both undertaken from Carthage a few years before 400 B.C. One, led by King Hanno, sailed around the coast of north and west Africa as far as the Gulf of Guinea; and in a temple in Carthage Hanno left an inscription of his own, recording the event. The other, reported in a reliable Roman geographical textbook of the fourth century B.C., was led by Himilco. It sailed northwards, past Portugal and Spain, around Normandy, and then on until it reached the *insula Albionum*—that is, the British Isles. Carthage no doubt became involved in the tin trade from Britain (in which the Greeks, too, later took part) as a result of this voyage.

The commercial stranglehold which the Phoenicians and their colonies—especially Carthage—exerted on the Mediterranean world inevitably led them into hostile contact with first

Minoan trade routes, shown in black, were mainly in the eastern half of the Mediterranean. Later, those of the Phoenicians and Carthaginians, shown in red, extended through the length and breadth of the Mediterranean and into the Red Sea and the Atlantic. There they ran far south along the West African coast and north to the British Isles and Frisian Isles.

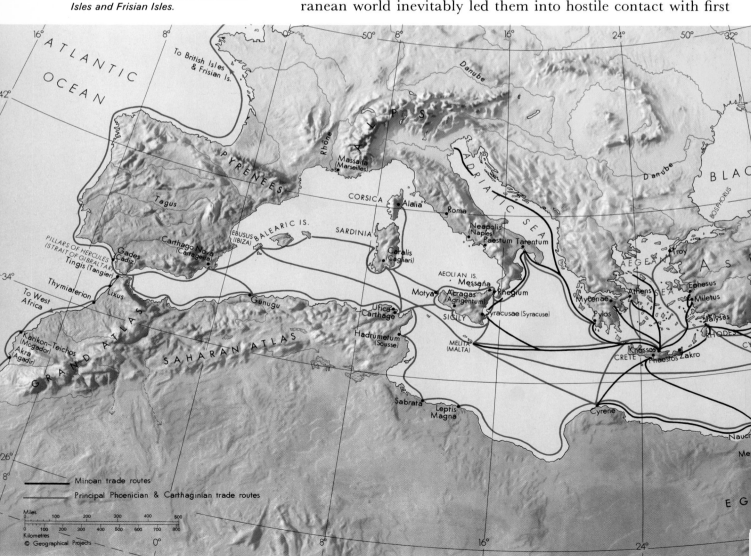

Minoan trade routes
Principal Phoenician & Carthaginian trade routes

Part of an inscription of about 400 B.C. commemorating the dedication of some gold plating to the god Reshef-Mikal. It uses the alphabetic script evolved in Phoenicia eight or more centuries earlier. This script greatly simplified the whole business of learning to read and write, so bringing literacy within reach of ordinary men and women.

the Greeks and then the Romans. Although Carthage was ultimately defeated and destroyed by the Romans, numerous benefits accrued to the emerging civilizations of the western Mediterranean as a result of this contact. Of these benefits one was supremely important—the alphabetic script.

The Phoenicians may have developed their script during the late Bronze Age (c. 1600–1200 B.C.), but the first clear inscription in it dates to about 1000 B.C. At this time it employed just 22 consonants and no vowels, the reader presumably being left to guess vowel sounds from context.

All the scripts of the great river valley civilizations consisted of hundreds or even thousands of characters, because a different character was needed for almost every object and idea, or in some cases for every syllable; and every one had to be memorized. The Phoenician alphabet, ancestor of all later alphabets, introduced an entirely new principle. By utilizing signs only for consonants (which, together with vowels, are the smallest units of speech) it reduced the number required to a mere handful, making it infinitely easier for people to learn to read and write—very important accomplishments among a people who lived largely by trade and commerce. Within two centuries of its appearance in Phoenicia, the Greeks had borrowed the alphabet and adapted it to write their own language. The great wealth of Greek literature that has been handed down to us is but one of the rewards.

The Phoenicians, like the Minoans, were not numerically strong, but the contribution of both to the world of their time was out of all proportion to their numbers. Both, with little land but comparatively long coastlines at their disposal, built up maritime civilizations that were largely dependent for their very existence on forging links with distant overseas lands. And by forging those links both of them passed on many of the fruits of their civilizations to other peoples and later times.

7
The Great Empires of Western Asia

Assyrian troops further their country's career of conquest by besieging another city. The ram arm of a siege machine batters the weak upper part of the walls. Shock troops swarm up scaling ladders. Slingers, trained to hurl their missiles with deadly accuracy, take aim at the city's defenders.

In the eighth century B.C., long before Phoenician colonies such as Carthage had become powerful in their own right, the cities of Phoenicia itself were being forced to pay tribute to the Assyrian Empire. Three centuries later the very existence of the Greek city-states was threatened by the Persian Empire. And for a short period, between the decline of the Assyrians and the rise of the Persians, a third considerable empire, known as the Neo-Babylonian or Chaldean Empire, also flourished in western Asia. Not only are the histories of all three linked but also their cultures, for each built largely on the earlier Sumerian and Babylonian civilizations.

The Assyrians first came into prominence around 1200 B.C. At that time the great surge of migrations and invasions through the Aegean and Asia Minor brought about the collapse of three Bronze Age empires—Egypt's empire in western Asia, the old Babylonian Empire and the Hittite Empire in Asia Minor. The homeland of the Assyrians, in northern Mesopotamia, stood at the meeting place of all three. For the next three centuries, the Assyrians themselves had a struggle to survive, but, thereafter, no longer hemmed in by powerful neighbours, they began to build up the first of western Asia's great Iron Age empires. First they gradually expanded their small kingdom and then, under King Assurnasirpal II (883-859 B.C.), embarked on a policy of conquest in every direction. Assurnasirpal and his successor, Shalmaneser III, extended Assyrian control over the whole of Mesopotamia and Syria, and among kings from farther afield who paid tribute to Assyria at this time was Jehu, king of Israel.

After the death of Shalmaneser III in 824 B.C., a succession of less able kings, a constant struggle for power within Assyria, and the growing strength of the Kingdom of Urartu in eastern Asia Minor, led to a period of relative weakness for Assyria. But from 746 B.C., when Tiglath-Pileser III came to the throne, Assyria went from strength to strength, until by 660 B.C., the

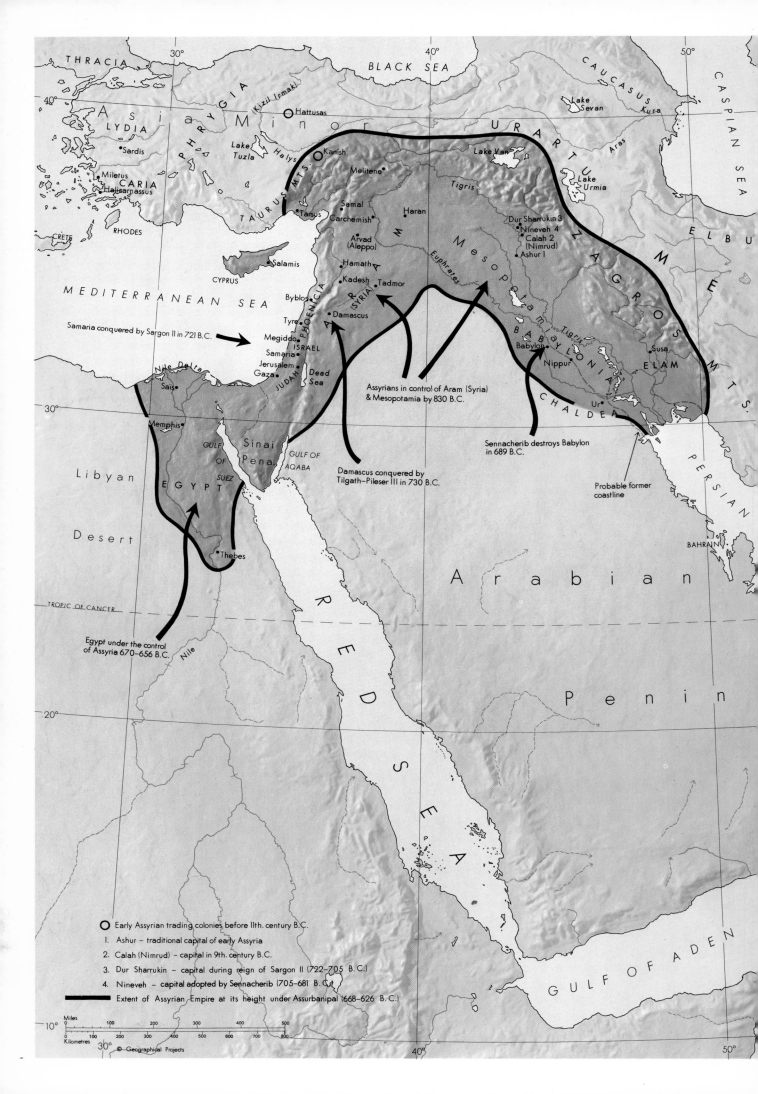

THRACIA
30°
BLACK SEA
40°
CAUCASUS
50°
CASPIAN SEA

Asia
LYDIA
Minor
PHRYGIA
(Kizil Irmak)
Hattusas
URARTU
ELBU
Lake Sevan
Kura
Aras

Sardis
Lake Tuzla
Halys
Kanish
Lake Van
Lake Urmia
ZAGROS
ME

Miletus
CARIA
Halisarnassus
Melitene
Tarsus
TAURUS MTS
Tigris
Mesopotamia
Dur Sharrukin 3
Nineveh 4
Calah 2
(Nimrud)
Ashur 1
M
RHODES

CRETE
Samal
Carchemish
Haran

Salamis
CYPRUS
Arvad (Aleppo)
Euphrates

MEDITERRANEAN SEA
Hamath
Kadesh
Tadmor
ARAM (SYRIA)
Babylonia
Tigris
ELAM
Susa

Samaria conquered by Sargon II in 721 B.C.
Byblos
PHOENICIA
Damascus
Babylon
Nippur

Tyre
Megiddo
ISRAEL
Samaria
Jerusalem
JUDAH
Gaza
Dead Sea
Assyrians in control of Aram (Syria) & Mesopotamia by 830 B.C.
CHALDEA
Ur
PERSIAN

Nile Delta
Sais
Memphis
GULF OF SUEZ
Sinai Pena
GULF OF AQABA
Sennacherib destroys Babylon in 689 B.C.

Libyan
EGYPT
SUEZ
Damascus conquered by Tilgath-Pileser III in 730 B.C.
Probable former coastline

Desert
Thebes
BAHRAIN

TROPIC OF CANCER
Arabian

Egypt under the control of Assyria 670–656 B.C.
Nile
Penin

RED SEA

20°

10°

GULF OF ADEN

○ Early Assyrian trading colonies before 11th. century B.C.
1. Ashur – traditional capital of early Assyria
2. Calah (Nimrud) – capital in 9th. century B.C.
3. Dur Sharrukin – capital during reign of Sargon II (722–705 B.C.)
4. Nineveh – capital adopted by Sennacherib (705–681 B.C.)
━━━ Extent of Assyrian Empire at its height under Assurbanipal (668–626 B.C.)

Miles
0   100   200   300   400   500
Kilometres
0   100 200 300 400 500 600 700 800
© Geographical Projects
30°
40°
50°

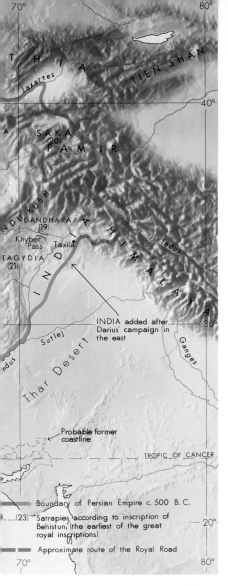

INDIA added after Darius' campaign in the east

Boundary of Persian Empire c. 500 B.C.

.....(23) Satrapies according to inscription of Behistun (the earliest of the great royal inscriptions)

Approximate route of the Royal Road

70° 80°

Above: The heavy red line shows the limits of the Persian Empire at its height, shortly before the death of Darius the Great in 486 B.C. Without stepping outside its bounds it was possible to make a journey longer than that from New York to San Francisco. The Royal Road from Susa to Sardis alone, marked as a broken red line, spanned a distance of some 1,600 miles (2,560 kilometres). The names of the empire's 23 satrapies at this time are shown with a number below them.

Left: Coins known as Persian archers, introduced by Darius the Great, showed the king grasping a bow. The gold coin, known to the Greeks as a daric, was 20 times as valuable as the silver one, which they called a siglos. The true Persian names are not known.

the unannounced visits of the inspector general, known as "the king's eye," who moved quickly from one satrapy to another along the royal roads. The laws which the satraps administered were often inscribed, in the language of the province, on a stone column which was set up where it could be read and consulted by the local people. This consideration for the subject peoples of the empire, which was characteristic of Persian rule at its best, also showed itself in religious toleration, and the Old Testament records that it was the Persians who allowed the Jews to return to Jerusalem from the exile into which the Babylonians had taken them.

Tolerance in matters of religion was probably essential, for the Assyrians and Babylonians, who had earlier controlled large areas that the Persians now held, had in general followed the religions which had persisted in Mesopotamia from very early times, and those religions still flourished. The Persians could not therefore have enforced adherence to their own very different religion without risking dangerous unrest. The gods the Persians worshipped were quite unknown in Mesopotamia. Supreme among them was Ahura-Mazda (Lord Wisdom), but there were others including Mithras, whose worship was later taken up and spread to Europe by the soldiers of Rome. At first the worship of these gods had been accompanied by bloody sacrifices, but by the time Persia became a great power a prophet named Zoroaster had begun to change all that. Zoroaster forbade blood offerings and preached the necessity for fair dealing and good deeds. His teachings came to be widely accepted, possibly during the reign of Cyrus the Great, and were reflected in the enlightened nature of Cyrus's government.

The Persians were not only tolerant; they also sought to improve the natural resources of their provinces—notably by transplanting crops from one area to another. It was in this way that the pistachio nut was introduced to the state of Aleppo, rice to Mesopotamia and sesame to Egypt. General prosperity and well-being were further enhanced by the introduction of coinage throughout the empire. Small silver coins had appeared in Asia Minor as early as the seventh century B.C., but it was not until a century later that King Croesus of Lydia introduced a true monetary system, with both gold and silver coins, into his kingdom. Some years after the Persian conquest of Lydia, Darius the Great adopted the idea. This introduction of a standard medium of exchange, together with the standardization of weights and measures, greatly stimulated trade.

Private banks emerged under this stimulus, offering loans, accepting deposits and investing in various enterprises. That of Murashshu and Sons, based at Nippur in Mesopotamia, invested in canals and in monopolies such as brewing; another, at Babylon, put money into housing, farmland, livestock and shipping. Investments in shipping may well have been profitable, for the Persians were the first great empire builders to place importance on naval affairs, and within the empire there were now ships of between 200 and 500 tons, capable of sailing between 60 and 80 miles (96 and 128 kilometres) a day. Ports were equipped with proper quays and fixed buoys for mooring, and sailors were graded strictly according to their skills.

Ships and their crews played a vital role in commerce, for the founding of the Persian Empire ushered in an era of trade on a scale, and over distances, never before known. Persian ships, partly manned by Phoenician crews, undertook voyages of exploration, while both raw materials and manufactured goods from India and Ceylon, Egypt and Greece, western and northern Europe were carried and traded throughout the empire and beyond it. At the same time, goods of all kinds flooded into the Persian treasuries in the form of annual tributes from the various parts of the empire.

Nowhere is the wealth and power of the Persian Empire better demonstrated than in Darius's own description of the building of his palace at Susa: "The cedar timber from there [Lebanon] was brought; the *yaka* timber was brought from Gandara and from Carmania. The gold was brought from Sardis and from Bactria. The precious stone lapis lazuli and carnelian . . . this was brought from Sogdiana. The . . . turquoise this was brought from Chorasmia. The silver and ebony were brought from Egypt. The ornamentation of the walls from Ionia was brought. The ivory . . . was brought from Ethiopia and from Sind and from Arachosia. The stone columns from Elam were brought."

Strangely, the wealth and power of the Persian Empire, and of the Assyrian and Neo-Babylonian empires which preceded it, did not stimulate a rash of new inventions and discoveries. And even where certain inventions and usages appear to be new we cannot always be sure that they were so, because archaeologists have here and there unearthed hints that they were in fact known earlier in Mesopotamia. For example, the Assyrians knew the use of several acids and salts, as well as mercury, sulphur and some metal oxides and sulphides; but there is no reason to think that all these were discovered, and first used, by the Assyrians. Similarly, the Assyrian records of eclipses, dating from the eighth century B.C., are the earliest that remain to us, but they were quite probably preceded by still earlier ones. Nevertheless, there seems little doubt that the astronomers of the Neo-Babylonian Empire were the first to give anything like precision to forecasting eclipses of the moon and the future positions of the planets. It is also likely that the Iron Age empires of western Asia were pioneers in studying plant and animal life at close quarters, for we know that the Assyrian and Neo-Babylonian kings promoted the construction of zoological gardens or game reserves, and the laying out of formal botanical gardens. In addition Nebuchadnezzar had a museum of a kind at Babylon, and Assurbanipal built up a famous library at Nineveh. In fact it was from the ruins of this library, where many historical records were stored, that archaeologists recovered vast quantities of cuneiform writings that now enable them to piece together a fairly complete history of the Babylonian and Assyrian civilizations.

Part of the great east stairway of the Apadana at Persepolis. Here, on the occasion of the New Year's Day celebrations, the highest dignitaries of the Persian Empire climbed the steps to the terrace, to watch tribute bearers from all 23 satrapies under Persian rule bring rich offerings to the king. Each offering represented the typical products of the land from which it came. Low-relief sculptures flanking the stairway realistically capture the flavour of the occasion. A detail from these reliefs, shown on the left, depicts tribute bearers from Lydia or Arabaya bringing bowls and vases.

In general, however, the contributions of the Assyrians, Babylonians and Persians to human progress should not be measured in terms of inventions or discoveries, but rather in terms of organization. Each of these empires exemplified the value of a well-oiled administrative machine which ran imperial affairs efficiently and profitably. The Assyrians were, perhaps, too harsh in their treatment of subject peoples to be really successful imperialists, even though their army enabled them to maintain an empire for longer than either the Babylonians or the Persians. But the Persians learned from the Assyrians' mistakes, and imposed a benevolent imperialism which showed the Greeks and the Romans how an empire could, and perhaps should, be run. Furthermore, they improved on the Assyrian administrative system in the management of both civilian and military affairs, and welded the wealth and commercial activities of all their provinces into a unified economy.

Alexander the Great was so impressed with what he saw and learned of the Persian Empire that he sought to blend Greek and Persian civilizations together. Perhaps no greater tribute could be paid to the empire that Cyrus founded.

8 The Civilization of Greece

The first Greek city-states were founded well after 800 B.C., at about the time when the Assyrian Empire was nearing its height. Less than three centuries later, when Persia's onslaughts on Greece were thwarted at Marathon and Salamis, Greek civilization was fast approaching its zenith. When Alexander the Great died in 323 B.C., having conquered the Persian Empire, the golden age of Greece was already past, and soon the Greek colonies in the western Mediterranean began to fall one by one into the hands of the Romans. The period of Greek greatness was not therefore immensely long. But the achievements of that period were tremendous.

When, and from where, the Greeks first came to Greece is still unknown, but they were almost certainly there by 2000 B.C. Treasures buried in the graves of warrior aristocrats at Mycenae, south of Corinth, soon after 1700 B.C., indicate that the Mycenaean civilization of the Greek mainland developed while the Minoan civilization was flowering in Crete, and owed not a little to it. After about 1450 B.C. the Mycenaean Greeks took over Minoan trade with western Asia and greatly expanded it. At the same time they established trading interests in the western Mediterranean. During the great invasions and migrations that wrought havoc throughout the east and central Mediterranean between about 1250 and 1150 B.C., Mycenae itself was destroyed, and the overseas contacts of mainland Greece were swept away.

The wave of destruction that put an end to Mycenaean civilization brought new peoples called Dorians to Greece from the north—peoples familiar with the use of iron. It also saw many Greeks fleeing across the Aegean to the relative safety of the coast of Asia Minor and its offshore islands. The history of Greece during the next few centuries, often called a "Dark Age," is almost unknown, and there is little evidence of continuity from the Mycenaean culture of the late Bronze Age.

In the agora of Athens a trio of men listens spellbound to a philosopher. In the partial shade of the stoas talk and trade go on side by side. In the background fine new temples and public buildings crown the rocky Acropolis.

84

Epidamnus

Lake Ochrida

Lake Prespa

Probable routes of the Dorians 1200–1000 B.C.

Vardar

Axios

PINDUS MTS

MACEDONIA

Pella

MT. OLYMPUS

Peneus

Tricca

Larissa

THESSALY

Crannon

Pharsalus

Pherae

PHTHIOTIS

Corcyra

CORFU

Ambracia

AMBRACIA

Leukas

LEUKAS

ACARNANIA

Achelous

Thermum

AETOLIA

AENIANIA MALIS

DORIS

LOCRIS

Heraclea

PHOCIS

Opus

Orchomenos

L. Copais

LOCRIS OZ

Naupaktos

Delphi

BOEOTIA

Thebes

Plataea

GULF OF CORINTH

AEGEAN

SEA

EUBOEA

SKYROS

NORTHERN SPORADES

Aeolian Greeks settle on Lesbos & the mainland after 1200 B.C.

LESBOS

Mytilene

KHIOS

Khios

Erythrae

Chalcis

Eretria

Marathon

Karystos

ATTICA

Athens

Piraeus

SALAMIS

Megara

MEGARA

Sicyon

Corinth

Aegium

ACHAEA

ANDROS

TENOS

KEA

Migration of the Ionian Greeks to Asia Minor after 1200 B.C.

ICARIA

SAMO

SERIPHOS

RHODOPE MTS

Maritsa

Maritsa

THRACE

Phrygians move south to Asia Minor

Maritsa

THASOS

SAMOTHRACE

IMBROS

Sestos

DARDA

Abydos

LEMNOS

Ilium (Troy)

Chalcidice

Olynthus

Potidaea

MT. ATHOS

IONIAN

ISLANDS

CEPHALONIA

ITHACA

ZACYNTHOS

Elis

ELIS

Olympia

Peloponnesus

ARCADIA

Mantinea

Tegea

ARGOLIS

Argos

IONIAN

SEA

Messene

MESSENIA

Sparta

SPARTA

KYTHERA

MEDITERRANEAN SEA

Dorians push south to Crete in 11th. century B.C.

SEA OF CRETE

NAXOS

SIPHNOS

MELOS

THERA

Dorians settle on Kos, Rhod & S.W. tip of Asia Minor

Cydonia

Khossos

Gortyna

CRETE

───── Boundaries of the city-states c. 500 B.C.

● Major Greek colonies established before 800 B.C.

○ Major Greek colonies established after 800 B.C.

Miles
0 10   20   30   40   50   60   70   80   90   100
0 10 20 30 40 50 60 70 80 90 100 110 120 130 140 150 160
Kilometres

© Geographical Projects

Left: Broken-line arrows show spread of Dorians from the north, first into Greece then into Crete and Asia Minor. Other arrows show migration of Aeolian and Ionian Greeks across the Aegean in the face of the advancing Dorians. Black dots mark Greek colonies established before 800 B.C., while open circles mark those established later. The Greek city-states had taken on the boundaries indicated by about 500 B.C.

Right: Head, chest and lower legs encased in plate armour, and carrying a round shield for further protection, the Greek hoplite, fighting shoulder to shoulder with his comrades, relied on his extremely long spear for attack.

But the heroic age of Mycenae was itself remembered, and described in the epic poetry handed down through the generations and eventually brought together by Homer in the great masterpieces of the *Iliad* and the *Odyssey*.

Homer wrote down the already old tales of Mycenae and its war with Troy towards the middle of the eighth century B.C., and by then the first Greek city-states had been founded on the mainland of Greece—at Sparta, Megara and Corinth—and on several islands off the coast of Asia Minor. The number of these states grew rapidly, and there was great rivalry between them to revive commercial contacts throughout the Mediterranean. Greek colonies were founded not only in the Aegean and the Black Sea but also in Sicily, Italy and the western Mediterranean, where the city-states found themselves in competition with the Etruscans and Phoenician colonists.

Although the Greeks as a whole were increasingly conscious of nationhood—of being a people distinct from those of the many other lands with which they were in contact—and though they could occasionally unite against a foreign foe, their first loyalty was to their own particular city. And intercity rivalry for colonies went hand-in-hand with diversity in forms of

87

Above: Greek red-figure vase of about 460 B.C., showing Apollo playing a lyre. The artist painted the whole background black, leaving the figure to show in the natural red of the clay. He then lined in the details of the figure.

government. At different times most city-states tried out various forms of government with varying degrees of success: monarchy, oligarchy (rule by a small exclusive group), and tyranny (rule—sometimes harsh but sometimes beneficent—by a man who had made himself dictator). Sparta was unusual in that it remained a monarchy long after most other states had turned to different forms of government. Under its kings Sparta grew powerful enough in the sixth century B.C. to control the whole of the Peloponnesus, the great peninsula south of the Gulf of Corinth. During much of that century Athens was ruled by tyrants, and it was not until 510 B.C. that the last of them was overthrown with the help of Sparta. It was then that Athens introduced a constitution under which all citizens had equal political rights and voted to elect representatives from whom a governing council was chosen by lot. Under this democratic form of government—named from the Greek word for people, *demos*—Athens' citizens were imbued with new civic pride, and its army and navy reorganized, just in time to meet and defeat Persia at Marathon in 490 B.C. and to join with the other Greeks in repulsing a second Persian attack ten years later.

The Athenian fleet played a major role in this second war, and from then on Athens became the dominant sea power in the Aegean. She then gradually built up an empire there and, under her leading statesman, Pericles, her greatest age began. Sparta meanwhile remained the preeminent land power in the Greek world, and the intense rivalry that grew up between the two states eventually led to the Peloponnesian War, the crucial phase of which occupied the years between 431 and 401 B.C. The war ended with Athens defeated, but with Sparta also

weakened. Yet the rivalry continued for the next half century, allowing Philip, king of Macedonia, to achieve his aim of expanding his small northern kingdom. He developed a highly trained citizen army with which he finally brought the whole of Greece under his control. In 337 B.C., having formed a federal union of all Greeks, allied with Macedonia, Philip declared war on Persia. But in the following year he was assassinated, and it was left to his son, Alexander the Great, to compass the downfall of the Persian Empire.

The highest achievements of most earlier civilizations are displayed in gigantic buildings and the rich burials of princes and kings. Those of ancient Greece are to be found in written works, fine sculpture and exquisite pottery. Greek vases are as highly prized today as they were in antiquity, particularly the red-figured pottery produced in Attica. These and painted vases show episodes from Greek mythology, legend and contemporary drama, or picture the athletic events, dancing and drinking that played a large part in everyday life. They were produced by potters and painters who often signed their names on the vases, and whose unsigned works we can identify by their style and technique.

The works of individual sculptors of the fifth century B.C. can be similarly identified. Monumental sculpture began in Greece in the later seventh century B.C. and a century later

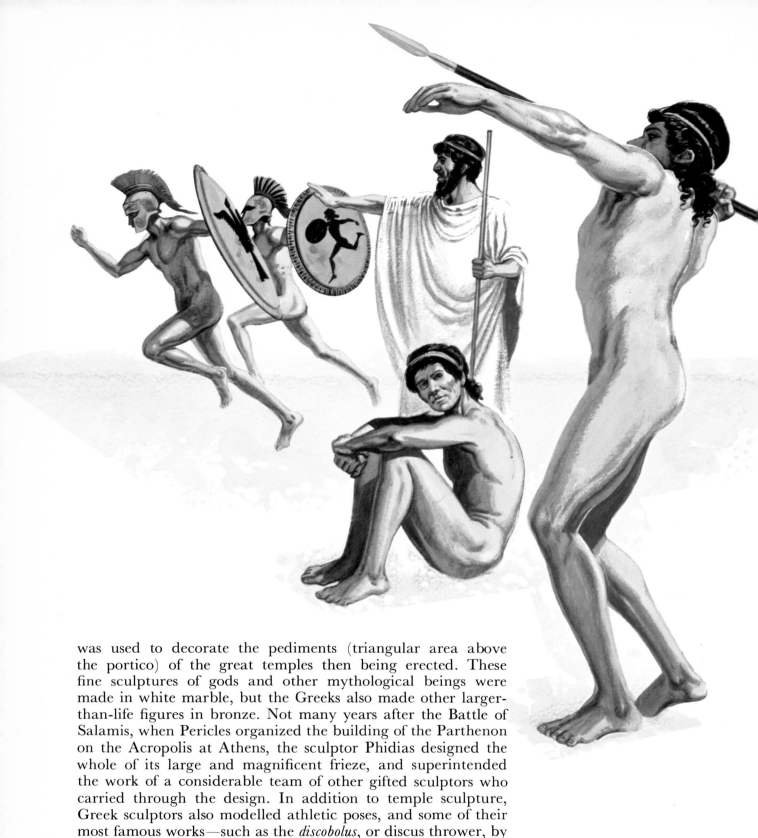

was used to decorate the pediments (triangular area above the portico) of the great temples then being erected. These fine sculptures of gods and other mythological beings were made in white marble, but the Greeks also made other larger-than-life figures in bronze. Not many years after the Battle of Salamis, when Pericles organized the building of the Parthenon on the Acropolis at Athens, the sculptor Phidias designed the whole of its large and magnificent frieze, and superintended the work of a considerable team of other gifted sculptors who carried through the design. In addition to temple sculpture, Greek sculptors also modelled athletic poses, and some of their most famous works—such as the *discobolus*, or discus thrower, by the sculptor Myron—were of this sort.

The Greeks were enthusiastic athletes, and their calendar included several important athletic contests, of which the best known today are the Olympic Games, begun, according to tradition, in 776 B.C. There were ten major events at the Greek Olympics, including a pentathlon comprising the long jump, the sprint, wrestling, the javelin and the discus. Sculptors made statues of athletes, pottery painters depicted them on vases, and the names of some of them are still known to us.

Athletes train for the Olympic Games, greatest occasion in the Greek sporting calendar, marked by a cessation of all hostilities between the oft-warring city-states. Held once in four years from 776 B.C. onwards, the Games were at first confined to running and wrestling but later included ten major events. So keen was interest that sculptors and potters immortalized athletes in stone and on vases, while a list of champions over a period of 500 years is still preserved.

90

It is clear both from the sculptures and the painted vases that the Greeks knew a great deal about human anatomy, especially the muscular system, much of which they learnt from their interest in athletics. In other fields of medicine, too, they rapidly developed both theory and practice in the period from about 550 B.C. onwards. Alcmaean, for example, dissected animals, studying elementary physiology and embryology. Democedes, a doctor from Croton, gained so great a reputation that he was hired not only by the state of Athens but even by Darius of Persia. But the greatest all-round medical man was the famous Hippocrates of Kos (c. 460–377 B.C.)—who gave his name to the oath taken for centuries by medical students. He insisted that a doctor's place was at the patient's bedside, and set new standards in the careful observation of symptoms and in finding a rational explanation for them. A casebook recording the course of actual illnesses is attributed to him, and his treatise on epilepsy—generally regarded as both sensible and accurate—still survives.

Other fields of science were also enthusiastically studied by the Greeks, and new contributions made in all of them. Many Greeks of the later fifth century B.C. were men of extremely wide learning. Protagoras studied ethics, politics, metaphysics and mathematics. Democritus, a philosopher first and foremost, also wrote on physics, mathematics, music, poetry, logic and psychology! This remarkable man propounded an atomic theory of the universe, suggesting that all matter was made up of minute indivisible particles. He also began the study of solid geometry, successfully calculating the volumes of pyramids and cones. Of more immediate practical importance, technical advances included the invention of the lathe, by Theodorus of Samos, and of iron welding by Glaukos of Khios.

The very fact that we know the names of these men points to an important contrast between Greek civilization and those that preceded it. In most earlier civilizations the state was all important, and the only names considered worth recording were those of kings, priests, governors and high military commanders. In Greece, and particularly in democratically governed Athens, every individual counted, and was worthy of mention if he proved himself outstanding in any field of human endeavour. In that atmosphere, Greek writers concerned themselves with science and scientists, inventions and inventors, art and artists, and a host of other matters that scribes in the civilizations of the Near East would never have thought of writing about. Thus Greek literature ranges over a wider field of human thought, interest and experience than any before it.

In particular the Greeks were the first people to write about philosophy as we now understand the word. In the sixth and fifth centuries B.C. men such as Pythagoras and Anaxagoras were much concerned with the definition of physical realities, and of mind and matter. Others were concerned with the nature of Truth, and how to perceive it, whether by the use of reason or by way of the senses. The first great Athenian philosopher, Socrates (469–399 B.C.), developed no formal doctrine and wrote nothing; yet he was greatly respected, and several later schools of philosophy regarded him as their founder. One of his pupils, Plato, wrote a great deal and also taught systematically, founding his famous Academy in 387 B.C. Although possibly the best known early school of higher education—roughly the equivalent of a modern university—Plato's Academy was not the first institution of its kind. A similar one had been founded a little earlier by Isocrates, who, like Plato, recognized the importance of education in the progress and betterment of the state. The greatest of Plato's pupils was Aristotle (c. 384–322 B.C.). He wrote on politics, philosophy, ethics, economics and natural history, and his works greatly influenced European thought throughout the Middle Ages.

L ong before Isocrates and Plato founded their educational centres, Athenian scholars had charged fees to teach not only philosophy but also the art of rhetoric (eloquence). This was because from 508 B.C. onwards, when Athens became a democracy, the magistrates who held the chief offices of state were directly responsible to the people, and dependent on their votes; they therefore needed to be able to make speeches that would convince people of the wisdom and correctness of their actions, and they were quite prepared to pay substantial fees to learn how to do so effectively.

Democracy necessarily implied the right of free speech—and full opportunity to criticize the government—at political gatherings. The same freedom spilled over on to the stage in the theatre, as in the comedies of Aristophanes (c. 445–385 B.C.) which criticize Athens' conduct of the Peloponnesian War.

T heatrical performances were not, of course, a wholly new Greek invention. There is reason to believe that a thousand years and more before the time of Aristophanes the Minoans had staged performances that included music, dancing and religious chanting in the courts of their palaces. But Greek theatre went far beyond performances of that kind. The Greeks developed two forms of true drama, the tragedy and the comedy, and in time staged drama contests and festivals.

The first Athenian tragedy was produced in 534 B.C., and from the very beginning Greek tragedy was concerned with the religious life both of the individual and of the state in which he lived. In the earlier tragedies, such as those of Aeschylus (c. 525–456 B.C.), the dominant role was taken by the chorus. Later the chorus declined in importance, and the great tragedian Sophocles (c. 496–406 B.C.) introduced far more dialogue, thereby developing Greek drama in the direction of theatre as we understand the term today. It was while Sophocles was writing, perhaps, that painted scenery was first used in a Greek theatre, and it was at the same period, too, that comedy first made its mark. Religious dances, mimes and revels had been performed for centuries before this, but it was the comedies of Epicharmus—the first produced about 486 B.C.—which presented comedy as a form of theatre in its own right, with its own plots and conventions. These early comedies

were a mixture of burlesque and parody, in which neither gods nor men were spared the writer's wit. The later comedies of Aristophanes concentrated their humour more on men than gods, and spared no one, from slaves and prostitutes to philosophers and magistrates.

Aristophanes, who was writing at the time of the Peloponnesian War, was a contemporary of Thucydides, one of the two great Greek historians. The other was Herodotus of Halicarnassus who lived in the earlier part of the fifth century B.C. Earlier chroniclers had been content merely to set down a sequence of events, but these two men introduced new dimensions into the writing of history. Herodotus travelled very widely within the known world, and his history is concerned with Egypt and the civilized world of western Asia as much as with Greek lands. Never content merely to learn facts, but determined to enquire and probe, and above all to ask why, he accumulated a great fund of knowledge wherever he went. From the fibres of all this information he spun the threads of many tales which he then wove together into a history. Where two or more different versions of the same story were current, Herodotus would faithfully record them all.

Thucydides was a historian of a different kind altogether. Much more concerned with contemporary events in Greece— particularly political matters and the Peloponnesian War—than

Theatres, like that at Delphi, above, were an entirely new feature of Greek town planning. They were located on a hill slope where rising tiers of seats could be sited to overlook a flat space. It was in such theatres that the world's first true tragedies and comedies were staged. The tragic and comic masks on the left are typical of those which actors donned for the performance. The players below all wear comic masks for a comedy in which Aristophanes aims his barbed humour at the frailties of men and women in all walks of life.

with handed-down accounts of earlier Near East history, he was scrupulously impartial, collecting together all the reliable information he could find, and then trying to interpret it. He believed that history repeats itself, and aimed to give others an understanding of what happened in history and why.

By the time Thucydides was writing, the first formally planned Greek cities had already been built. The earliest such cities we know of are Miletus and the port of Athens at Piraeus, both of which, according to tradition, were planned by Hippodamus of Miletus. At Miletus a right-angled grid of streets divided the town into a series of housing blocks of regular size. In the centre of the town space was left for the principal public, commercial and religious buildings, which were gradually erected over a long period. The same sort of planning was employed at Olynthus in about 430 B.C., and at Priene some 80 years later. The size of the housing blocks, and the number of houses in each block, varied from one city to another. At Olynthus there were ten houses to a block, all of similar type with a central courtyard; at Priene there were only four houses in a block and they were far more varied in plan.

Among the public buildings in a typical Greek city were several of a kind unknown in the cities of other ancient civilizations. At the very centre of everyday life was the *agora*, which served both as a marketplace and a place of assembly for the people. Around it were open-sided halls called *stoas*, their roofs supported by colonnades, which were simply used as places to meet and talk—about business, politics, philosophy or anything else. Also grouped around or near the *agora* were the temples, impressively beautiful in their simplicity, together with the council hall, altars and law courts. All these buildings were completely accessible to the citizens, not hidden away in sacred or royal enclosures and citadels as in the cities of the Near East, India and China. The other major public buildings were the theatre and the gymnasium. The former was an entirely new

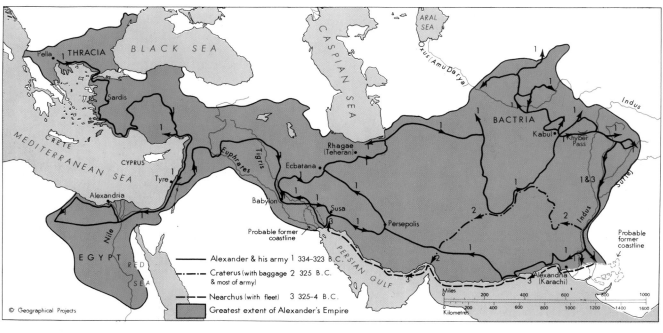

© Geographical Projects

Alexander & his army 1 334–323 B.C.
Craterus (with baggage 2 325 B.C. & most of army)
Nearchus (with fleet) 3 325–4 B.C.
Greatest extent of Alexander's Empire

Despite the ravages of 2,500 years, the damage from an explosion that rocked it in 1687, and the removal of much of its sculpture to Britain in 1812, the Parthenon, with its noble array of Doric columns, is still a fitting monument to the glory that was Greece.

Map showing the maximum extent of the gigantic empire that Alexander the Great built during the years 334 to 323 B.C. In that brief time Greek influence was extended eastwards to beyond the Indus and southwards to the desert fringe of Nubia. Black lines show routes followed by troops under Alexander during a campaign that left "no more worlds to conquer," and by those under two of his commanders, Craterus and Nearchus, on their journey back to Persia.

feature of town planning, and its location was determined by the availability of a hill slope where rising, circular tiers of seats could be sited to overlook a stage and a semi-circular orchestra, as the Greeks called the flat space before the stage building. The gymnasium, with its halls and colonnaded court, was essentially a school, but it also offered facilities for athletic exercises for all.

The buildings and the planning of Greek cities reflect the most attractive features of Greek life. The dignity and restraint of the architecture, and the importance given to buildings designed for the education and pleasure of the population as a whole, emphasize the cultural enlightenment of the Greeks; and the built-in freedom of movement within the city underlines the political and personal freedom which the Greeks held so dear. When that freedom was eventually taken from them by the Romans, the Greeks still had an important role to play in the development of the world's culture, for the Romans adopted and adapted much of what was best in Greek civilization and carried it westwards to Italy and eventually to the empire they were creating throughout the Mediterranean and beyond.

9 The Civilization of Rome

It is A.D. 130, and Rome, no longer bent on further conquest, concentrates on defence. Here, Roman legionaries arrive for a long spell of duty on Hadrian's Wall, the vast complex of stone wall, forts and turrets recently built on the empire's far frontier in the wilds of Britain.

Rome was far from being a world power when Greece was enjoying its golden age, and by the time Alexander the Great founded his empire, the city still ruled only a narrow strip of land between the west coast of Italy and the Apennine mountains. But in time Rome was to win an empire surpassing even that of Alexander, an empire including Mesopotamia, Egypt, Crete, Phoenicia and Greece as well as much of western Europe, to which she would bring the fruits of civilization.

Long after their city had achieved greatness, the Romans developed a tradition that it had been founded in 753 B.C. by Romulus, a descendant of the Trojan prince Aeneas who fled from Troy after its destruction by the Greeks. But in fact little is known about Rome in its formative years except that it was ruled by kings, and that from 616 to 510 B.C. those kings were Etruscans—men of the civilization that flourished in a broad area just to the north of Rome. The Etruscans had close trading contacts with the Greeks and adopted many features of Greek culture, including architectural styles, grid layouts for cities and an alphabet probably based on the Greek. The Romans, in turn, learned much from the Etruscans.

But Rome was not content to remain permanently under Etruscan rule. In 510 B.C. its citizens revolted, banished the last Etruscan king, and set up an independent republic. Then for more than a century Rome had to struggle to maintain her independence in the face of widespread hostility—from Etruscans to the north, Latins to the south, Samnites to the southeast. She survived, however, and as time passed began to extend first her influence and then her control over the neighbouring cities and states of central Italy. By 282 B.C. Greek colonists in southern Italy recognized the threat she presented, and sought help from Greece. Pyrrhus of Epirus came to their aid with 25,000 men, but in vain. The Roman troops defeated his army and then went on to conquer the whole Italian peninsula.

Rhine
Lake
Constance
Rhône
PENNINE
ALPS
Maggiore
Simplon Pass
Gt. St. Bernard Pass
Little St.
Bernard Pass
A L P S
San Bernardo
Pass
RHAETIAN ALPS
Inn
Brenner Pass
HOHE TAUERN
NIEDERE TAUERN
Drava
Lake
Balaton
Sava
Siscia
(Sisak)
Drava
Danube
MARITIME
ALPS
Augusta
Taurinorum
(Turin)
Po
Comum
(Como)
Mediolanum
(Milan)
Cremona
Placentia
(Piacenza)
Parma
Garda
Verona
Patavium
(Padua)
Opitergium
Aquileia
Tergeste
(Trieste)
Istria
Hatria
(Adria)
Po
Mutina
(Modena)
Bononia
(Bologna)
Ravenna
Genua
(Genoa)
A
P
E
N
Luna
Caesena
Rubicon
Ariminum
(Rimini)
Pisaurum
(Pesaro)
Ancona
ILLYRI
Salonae
LIGURIAN SEA
Pisae
(Pisa)
Florentia
(Florence)
ETRURIA
Perusia
(Perugia)
L. Trasimeno
Clusium
(Chiusi)
Tiber
Firmum
N
I
N
Spoletium
(Spoleta)
ADRIATIC SEA
ELBA
L. Bolsena
Epidaurus
CORSICA
Alalia
Tarquinii
ROME
LATIUM
E
S
Sipontum
Ostia
SAMNIUM
Beneventum
(Benevento)
Barium
(Bari)
Tarracina
Capua
Brundisium
(Brindisi)
SARDINIA
VESUVIUS
Salernum
(Salerno)
Neapolis
Pompeii
ISCHIA
CAPRI
Paestum
Tarentum
(Taranto)
TYRRHENIAN
Buxentum
Thurii
SEA
Croton
(Crotone)
Carales
(Cagliari)
Scylacium
AEOLIAN IS.
(LIPARI IS.)
Messana
(Messina)
Panormus
(Palermo)
Rhegum
(Reggio di Calabria)
STRAIT OF MESSINA
IONIAN
SEA
SICILIAN CHANNEL
Motya
Lilybaeum
(Marsala)
MT.
ETNA
Catana
(Catania)
SICILY
Agrigentum
(Agrigento)
Syracusae
(Syracuse)
Hippo Regius
(Annaba)
Utica
C. Bon
PANTELLERIA
AFRICA
Carthage
MELITA
(MALTA)

Miles
0 25 50 75 100 125 150
0 25 50 75 100 125 150 175 200 225
Kilometres
© Geographical Projects

Roman Republic before Punic Wars
Boundary of Latium
Principal Roman roads
● Former Greek colonies

At that time, Rome had a long-standing treaty with Carthage by which each agreed to respect the sphere of influence of the other. But in 264 B.C., Rome was asked to intervene in the affairs of Sicily, and at once Rome and Carthage found themselves in conflict. The event marked the beginning of the Punic Wars between Rome and Carthage, which lasted intermittently from 264 to 146 B.C. and saw the foundations of the Roman Empire firmly laid, though it was not yet called an empire.

The first defeat of Carthage led to the establishment of Rome's first overseas province, Sicily, in 227 B.C. In the Second Punic War, when Hannibal repeatedly beat Roman armies but could not take Rome itself, Rome also opened war against Macedonia, whose king attempted to help Hannibal. In 146 B.C., the year in which Carthage was finally defeated and razed to the ground, the Roman provinces of Macedonia and Africa (central north Africa) were formed. The conquest of the Mediterranean basin was virtually completed with the formation of the province of Asia (western Asia Minor) in 113 B.C. By that time the first Roman province north of the Alps had already been established and Rome was beginning the conquest of Europe.

In Republican Rome government rested essentially in the hands of the senate, an elected assembly first of 100, later of 300, men. But as conquests abroad continued, struggles for personal power within the senate developed at home. These usually involved successful military commanders, some of whom were also successful businessmen. In 60 B.C. three such powerful men—Pompey, Crassus and Julius Caesar—joined forces and agreed to share the control of the Roman state between them. Seven years later, when Crassus was murdered, Pompey was encouraged to extend his own power at the expense of Caesar,

who was then busy with the conquest of Gaul (present-day France). So in 49 B.C. Caesar crossed the river Rubicon, returned to Rome, and, with his superior forces, made successful war on Pompey and established himself as sole ruler of the Roman world. He accepted the title of dictator, but although he refused the offer of kingship many thought he intended to restore the monarchy, and this led to his assassination in 44 B.C.

Caesar's will appointed his nephew, Octavian, as his heir, but the appointment was bitterly contested by Mark Antony—once Caesar's lieutenant—with the backing of a strong armed force. Only after a prolonged struggle did Octavian emerge in 30 B.C. as the new ruler of Rome. Then, by subtly manipulating the senate, he managed to extend his power and perpetuate his position. In 27 B.C. he was given the title Augustus (the Majestic One), and founded the long line of emperors who were thenceforth to rule the Roman Empire. The early emperors continued to expand their overseas territories—a process which gave the army an even more important role than it had already played in Roman affairs. As its importance grew, so did its political power. In A.D. 41 the army intervened directly in politics at the highest level—first to assassinate the existing emperor and then to choose his successor. The example set on this occasion was to be followed on many others, and inevitably led to the bitter struggles between rival claimants to the throne which did so much harm to the empire in its later years.

Towards the end of the third century A.D., after one such period of political strife, the emperor Diocletian decided that the empire was too large to be satisfactorily controlled by one man, and created a second emperor, Maximian, to share the responsibility with him. Later, in A.D. 326, the emperor Constantine began the erection of a second capital at Constantinople, on the site of the ancient city of Byzantium, and in A.D. 335 it was decided that when he died the empire should be split between his heirs. It was briefly united again towards the end of the fourth century, but by A.D. 400 it had once more been divided—this time finally.

By that time the defences of the Western Empire were crumbling in the face of invading hordes. In 406 the Romans found they could no longer hold their lengthy Rhine frontier, and three years later Britain was told it must look to its own defence. Rome itself was taken and sacked by the Visigoths the very next year. Although some semblance of order was briefly restored, the Western Empire had virtually ceased to exist. The last emperor of Rome was deposed in 476, leaving what remained of Rome's glory to be maintained by the emperors of the Eastern, or Byzantine, Empire at Constantinople.

One reason for the collapse of the Western Empire was the declining quality of the troops defending it. By the late fourth century many of the army units in Gaul, Germany, and Britain were recruited entirely from barbarian peoples beyond the empire's frontiers, and even the legions were no longer the superb fighting machines they had been in the late first and early second centuries A.D.

Roman troops building a road. With no tar or bitumen available, the surface will be of rammed gravel, and the sides are flanked by drainage ditches to protect it from too great an accumulation of water. The road may often need resurfacing, but its foundation of large stones will last centuries.

At that time, the Roman army—now a regular army—was the finest fighting force the world had seen. Its backbone, and its elite, were between 20 and 30 legions, consisting of soldiers who were Roman citizens. Each legion comprised between 5,000 and 6,000 men, of whom just over 5,000 were actual combatants, the rest being engineers, surveyors, clerks, medical personnel, smiths and other specialists. Each legion was divided into cohorts, and each cohort into six centuries (a century consisting of 80 men, not 100 as the name suggests). Every cohort was commanded by an officer called a tribune, and every century was under the immediate command of a centurion. The discipline these officers and N.C.O.'s instilled in the legionaries, and the regular drill and weapons practice they insisted on, paid off handsomely on the field of battle.

To assist the legions, and to help garrison the conquered provinces, auxiliary units were recruited from the noncitizen population of the empire. These units included infantry and cavalry as well as such specialists as archers. In later times other army units were formed of men from allied or tributary states beyond the frontiers; and eventually even barbarian soldier

settlers—who were given land to farm in exchange for liability
to military service when required—were also used to bolster the
empire's defences.

Unlike these late comers to Rome's forces, the legionaries and
auxiliaries lived in permanent forts which they themselves built
to a more or less standardized pattern. At the centre was the
headquarters building, flanked by the commander's house and
granaries that could hold a year's supply of grain. One or two
workshop buildings were also in the central area. On either side
of these buildings were the barrack blocks—long buildings
fronted by a covered verandah and with rows of double rooms,
each one occupied by eight or ten men. At one end more
spacious quarters housed the centurions. Through the centre of
the fort, laid out at right angles to one another, ran two main
streets which led to the four main gateways.

Beyond the gates at least one of the streets would link up with
a roadway, for most of the major roads in a Roman
province were initially built by the army, mainly for its own use.
Routes were carefully surveyed by army surveyors, and roads
usually ran in a series of straight stretches. The major roads,
about 27 feet (8.2 metres) wide, were flanked by drainage
ditches. Good drainage was essential, for the Romans had no tar
or bitumen for road surfacing, and the rammed gravel they
used could easily be churned up if too much water accumulated

The triple tier of arches of the Pont du Gard, near Nîmes, France, still dominates the surrounding landscape. Built by the Romans, its function was to bring a plentiful supply of free water into the city from 25 miles (40 kilometres) away.

on it. However, the large-stone foundations on which the gravel rested ensured that the whole road did not break up and become unusable; and roads were frequently repaired and resurfaced.

Major roads, apart from serving the needs of the army, were also used by the Imperial Post. About every 25 miles (40 kilometres) along the Imperial Post routes rest houses called *mansiones* were built, where government messengers and officials could obtain overnight accommodation, as well as fresh horses. Often small towns grew up around these posting stations, and in the larger towns along the routes public inns provided accommodation for travellers.

The building of good, well-surfaced roads also meant that large carts could now carry farm produce in a reasonable time to towns several miles away, where there were sizeable markets for their loads. This encouraged farmers throughout Roman-occupied Europe to begin growing more food than they and their families could eat, in order to sell the excess at a profit. Some used the profits to build Romanized farmhouses or villas.

Other Roman contributions to the development of European farming included sound advice on estate management and the introduction of new tools, such as the iron-tipped spade and the scythe. The Romans also encouraged the growing of several new crops, including cabbages, parsnips, turnips, carrots, rye, oats and various fruit trees. Reaping, however, was still done by hand, although in Gaul, at least, a harvesting machine was built and used on a limited scale. However, the Romans did develop and spread the use of the watermill for grinding grain, although it is unlikely that they actually invented it.

Conquest and the resulting new sources of slave labour meant that the Romans themselves never had any strong incentive to discover new sources of power. This is one of the reasons industrial development in the empire was relatively limited. Many industries remained local crafts and family businesses, and large factories were unusual. The most obvious exceptions are the famous potteries of Gaul, which produced finely made and decorated red pottery known as Samian ware, exported throughout the western part of the empire. Other potteries found sufficient favour to become major producers within their own province or region, and some of them must have employed many people.

Some of the smaller local potteries also produced bricks and tiles for public and private building. Baked bricks were not, of course, a Roman invention, but Roman bricks were fired at 1000° C as compared with about 600° C for Egyptian bricks, and as a result they were far more durable and less porous. These bricks, the use of cement and the introduction of a form of concrete made of cement mixed with brick rubble enabled the Romans to build in ways previously unknown. The brick-and-concrete arch and the brick-faced, concrete-cored wall, combined with the use of cranes, pulleys, cogs and levers, allowed them to erect domed and vaulted buildings of massive size and exceptional strength, as well as arched structures like their famous aqueducts.

Roman coinage was used throughout the empire, even for minor business transactions. The Roman relief at the top of the page shows peasants of northwest Europe bringing their rents to a collector and his staff. The relief above shows a cloth merchant displaying his goods.

The provision of a plentiful supply of free water was but one of many public amenities of a developed Roman town. At Roman Lyons in France, four aqueducts brought in some 17 million gallons of fresh water daily. This was used in public fountains and baths as well as in some private houses. The small admission fee the baths normally charged purchased not only the pleasures of dry heat, steam heat and wet bathing, but also the opportunity for exercising, gambling, chatting or talking business in comfort and comparative luxury. Free

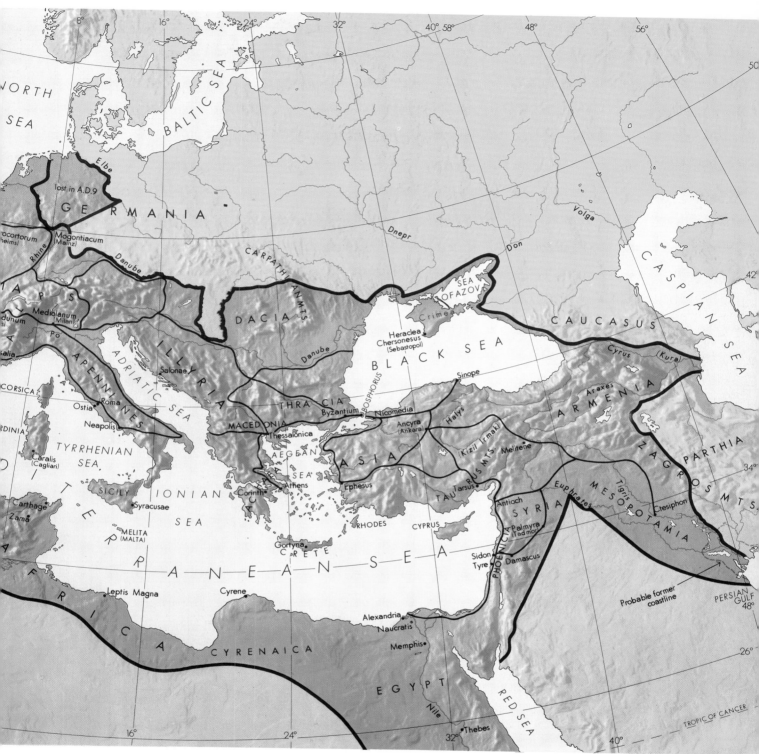

Map showing the Roman Empire at its height, soon after A.D. 100. It embraced many of the homelands of earlier civilizations—Mesopotamia, Egypt, Crete, Phoenicia and mainland Greece— all of which contributed directly or indirectly to Rome's own culture. That culture it spread far northwards and westwards across Europe.

entertainment in the theatre or amphitheatre was also offered on the many public holidays which the Roman world celebrated. At the former, musical or dramatic performances were produced, while the latter was the scene of more energetic spectacles—acrobatics, wild animal displays and gladiatorial combats. The more important cities might also boast a circus where horse and chariot races took place. The Circus Maximus at Rome could accommodate an audience of over a quarter of a million people for such events!

Many of the people in that gigantic audience would have lived in the blocks of five- and six-storey tenements that were a feature of Rome, Ostia and other large Italian cities—especially in the first and second centuries A.D. These blocks eased the massive housing problems which Rome faced. With large windows overlooking paved and well-drained streets, their five- or six-room apartments were probably not unpleasant homes in which to live. But they could not compare with the homes of the wealthy, either in Rome or in the provinces. These were often built on only one level, with the principal rooms arranged around an open court, usually laid out as a formal garden with flowers, shrubs and fountains. The house normally had its own bathing accommodation, and living rooms and bedrooms were paved with patterned or illustrated mosaics and had attractively painted or panelled walls. This type of house, originating in the warm lands around the Mediterranean, was copied by the wealthy throughout most of the Roman Empire, even in chilly northern Gaul and Britain. In those areas more emphasis was placed on centrally heated living rooms and bedrooms.

Luxurious Roman baths were not confined to metropolitan Rome. In its heyday this great public bath at Leptis Magna, in North Africa, offered all the amenities of the finest baths in Rome itself. Built during the reign of Emperor Hadrian, it was marble-floored and marble-walled, with vaults doubtless embellished with paintings.

In the provinces such houses were often owned by members of the tribal council, for the Romans allowed many conquered peoples local self-government. Thus although each province was run by a governor (who was usually a Roman senator) much of the day-to-day administration was in the hands of native peoples. Their tribal councils were patterned on the model of the Roman senate, and normally consisted of 100 members from whom magistrates were elected for an annual term of office. These not only saw to local financial and fiscal affairs but were also responsible for administering local law.

Some of this would be concerned with matters within the towns themselves. The width of streets and height of buildings were subject to restrictions, and so, too, was the extent to which buildings could encroach upon the streets. But many of the cases coming up before the local magistrates were disputes in civil law, concerning inheritance, land tenure and fraud. Where a Roman citizen was involved these cases would be judged according to Roman law, which later became, and still remains, the basis for law in much of western Europe, though not in Britain; but where Roman citizens were not involved native

The amphitheatre offered the Roman populace the thrills of blood and death. Here a retiarius, armed with trident and net, does battle with a helmeted secutor, armed with sword and shield.

This Roman house at Pompeii, built around an open courtyard laid out as a formal garden, belonged to a wealthy banker. It has been restored to show how it looked before an eruption of Vesuvius engulfed the town in ash and lava in A.D. 79. In Rome and other large cities most poorer people lived in apartments.

law operated. Criminal law was administered solely by the provincial governor, who could sentence guilty parties to death, forced labour in mines, or various lesser penalties.

Some of Rome's greatest advocates, like Cicero (106–43 B.C.) and Pliny the Younger (A.D. 62–113), were also among her greatest writers, and left accounts not only of speeches they made in legal trials but also of much else that went on in their lifetimes. In addition we still have the writings of other Roman authors: historians like Livy (59 B.C.–A.D. 17) and Tacitus (c. A.D. 58–102), poets like Horace (65–8 B.C.) and Vergil (70–19 B.C.), and practical men like Julius Caesar (102–44 B.C.) and Vitruvius the architect (first century B.C.). Even more surprising than the survival of such writings to the present day is their wide availability during the Roman period itself. In the second century A.D. Rome had over two dozen public libraries, and many booksellers. The wealthier Roman could buy books for his own personal library, and even in far-off Britain we find quotations from, or illustrations of, Vergil's great poem the *Aeneid*, on walls or floors of wealthy homes.

Roman books were at first written on rolls of papyrus, as in Egypt, but these were cumbersome and in the time of the emperors leaves of vellum or parchment were stitched together to form books similar to those of today. Printing did not yet exist, but a step towards making books cheaper and more widely

available was taken by a friend of Cicero's called Pomponius. He employed one slave who read out the text of a book, and several more who copied it down at the same time.

The widespread popularity of these books in all parts of the empire attests the equally widespread use of the Latin language, at least among the educated classes of society, for pleasure as well as for business. Among these same classes Roman manners and customs, and the whole Roman way of life, were adopted with equal enthusiasm, and produced a certain uniformity of culture. At a less personal level the same was achieved by the universal use of Roman coinage, Roman weights and measures, Roman building techniques and architectural forms and Roman law. Yet within this uniformity the Romans allowed and even encouraged the survival of native traditions, and themselves adopted and adapted ideas from all parts of the empire.

No more vivid illustration of this can be given than the adoption, by Constantine, of Christianity as the official religion of the Roman Empire. In A.D. 312 the old Roman pantheon, derived like so much else in Roman civilization from that of the Greeks, was abandoned in favour of the monotheism propounded by an obscure Jewish carpenter called Jesus. In the centuries that followed, it was to be under His banner that the Roman Empire survived in the east and provided the vital link between the civilization of Rome and that of medieval Europe.

A mosaic representation of Emperor Justinian, in a church in Ravenna. After the Western Roman Empire had disintegrated, the Eastern Roman, or Byzantine, Empire survived. The greatest Byzantine emperor was Justinian (A.D. 527–65). During his reign Italy and North Africa were again brought under imperial rule.

10 Early Civilizations of America

The Romans believed that they ruled most of the world and knew about the rest. But they were just as ignorant of what lay beyond "Ocean"—the then-mysterious Atlantic—as were all the civilizations that preceded them. Traders and explorers travelled great distances by ship but usually kept as close to land as possible, and there is no reliable evidence to suggest that they ever ventured across either the Atlantic or the Pacific to set foot in the New World.

No one yet knows precisely when the first men arrived in America, but they were certainly there well before the end of the Ice Age. At that time a broad land bridge spanned the Bering Strait and part of the Bering Sea, and the people who first crossed it into western North America were doubtless hunters and food gatherers. In course of time their descendants spread far southwards and eastwards, and shortly after 10,000 B.C. there were hunters on the great plains of North America, in southern Mexico and along the chain of the Andes, possibly as far south as Patagonia. Those who inhabited the plains of North America remained hunters for thousands of years. But farther south there was a steady development towards a settled, agricultural existence, based on plants very different from those grown by the early farmers of the Old World. Recent investigations in the Teotihuacán Valley of Mexico have shown that cultivation began there, on a very small scale, perhaps as early as 6000 B.C.; and before 4000 B.C. maize and beans were being systematically grown to supplement food supplies which still came mainly from hunting and food gathering. But it was not until some time after 1000 B.C. that cultivated foods accounted for over half the food supply; this was achieved only by the introduction of irrigation.

By this time there were also farming communities farther south, in Peru, and they were already beginning to use metal—locally obtained gold. This they hammered into shape on stone

It is 1519. An Aztec war party returns with captives destined for sacrifice to the gods, who must be nourished with human hearts or the world may end. So the Aztecs must wage war, to provide the victims their gods demand.

moulds, decorating the finished articles with a punch. Yet several centuries were to pass before they learned the use of silver and copper and the art of casting metals. Nor were these early Peruvian farmers yet ready to take the steps which would lead them to civilization.

Instead, it was the Stone Age farmers of Mexico who first brought civilization to the New World. In the early centuries A.D. the Maya people of southern Mexico began to build ceremonial cities, in which well-built stone step-pyramids, topped by shrines, dominated the view, just as the Parthenon dominated Athens. Several centuries later they were building similar cities in Yucatan. The exterior walls of shrines were decorated with elaborate and skilfully carved stone reliefs, and inside there were colourful wall paintings showing priests, warriors, and—all too rarely—scenes from the everyday life of these remarkable people. Many of these monuments can be accurately dated, because the Maya had a system of hieroglyphic writing and a very accurate calendar, both of which we can partly understand. In addition, although they remained essentially a Stone Age people throughout their history, they developed a sophisticated numeral system which allowed them to count and calculate in millions. Indeed, such was their preoccupation with mathematical and calendrical calculations that some archaeologists estimate that they devoted a third of

Map labels:
GULF OF MEXICO
TROPIC OF CANCER
SA MADRE OF CANCER
TOLTECS move south to settle & rule from Tula
CHICHIMECA
La Quemada
S.A. MADRE ORIENTAL
Rio Grande de San Iago
TOLTEC
Pánuco
El Tajín
BAY OF CAMPECHE
Mayapán
Chichén Itzá
Ukmal
MAYA (MEXICAN PERIOD)
Tula Teotihuacán
Tenochtitlán L. Texcoco
Tlaxcala
AZTEC
Cholula
MIXTEC
Xochicalco
Tehuacán
Tres Zapotes
OLMEC
La Venta
Palenque
Piedras Negras
Tikal
GULF OF HONDURAS
Sierra Madre del Sur
Río de las Balsas
Monte Albán
Mitla
ZAPOTEC
Yaxchilán
MAYA (CLASSIC PERIOD)
Quiriguá
Motagua Copán
PACIFIC
OCEAN

Legend:
Major Mayan cities
Aztec capital
- - - Areas of some of the earlier (classic) civilisations: Olmec, Classic Monte Albán, Classic Teotihuacán
-·-·- Extent of Maya culture
⟶ Spread of Toltec influence after 10th. century
▬ Extent of Aztec Empire c. 1510
© Geographical Projects

Miles
0 50 100 150 200 250
Kilometres
0 50 100 150 200 250 300 350 400

Coordinate labels: 105°, 100°, 95°, 25°, 90°, 20°, 15°

Reddish tint shows areas tributary to the Aztecs about A.D. 1500. While such areas paid tribute to the Aztecs, they did not form a true centrally governed empire; and parts of southern Mexico, such as Tlaxcala and Cholula, remained almost wholly independent. Indeed, some of the earlier civilizations (named in capital letters), like the Maya and the Toltec, had probably been just as territorially powerful as were the Aztecs.

Left: Found near Tula, these figures, 15 feet (4·5 metres) tall, were carved as supports for a large temple roof. They are the work of the Toltecs, supreme in central and southern Mexico from A.D. 950 to 1150.

their time to such matters. This may well have been one of the factors that led to their gradual decline and the eventual abandonment of their ceremonial cities.

As the Maya civilization faded it was replaced by that of the Toltecs, who built on its foundation, introducing new crafts, including featherwork and the carving of jade and turquoise. Between about A.D. 950 and 1150 the Toltecs ruled much of central and southern Mexico from their capital at Tula, until they were supplanted by the Chichimec tribes, who became the inheritors of their culture. Among those tribes were the Aztecs, of very little importance then and still searching for an area of land to settle. They eventually occupied one of the few spots not already inhabited—a swampy island in Lake Texcoco. There, soon after A.D. 1300, they founded their capital of Tenochtitlán, and from it launched a series of raids on the other cities and peoples around the shores of the lake. Gradually, by military skill and sheer persistence, they began to exert control over their neighbours. By alliance with the stronger of them they then extended the area over which they wielded power, until by about 1500 they dominated most of southern and central Mexico.

This dominance, however, never took the form of a proper empire where all the peoples and states were ruled by a single monarch acting through a centralized administration. The Aztecs primarily sought, and demanded, tribute. From the

tributary peoples they received great quantities of precious materials of all sorts—jade, emeralds, gold, cacao, spices, the skins of wild animals and the feathers of rare birds. All these, and other raw materials, were taken to Tenochtitlán, where Aztec craftsmen used them to make jewellery, blankets and clothing for both everyday and ceremonial use, and ceremonial knives and swords with blades of obsidian—for although the Aztecs used metal for making jewellery they seldom used it for anything else.

An Aztec representation of ritual human sacrifice. Spanish chroniclers who saw such scenes have described one of the procedures commonly followed. The victim, possibly drugged, was thrown on his back on a flat stone before the door of a pyramid-top temple. His breast was then opened and his heart torn out. His heart was offered to the god and his body hurled down the pyramid steps.

The craftsmen who made such things, and the merchants who traded with distant lands, were valued members of Aztec society, ranking higher in the social scale than the peasants who worked the land and the slaves who were acquired by warfare and conquest. Of even higher status were the civil servants, the military knights and the priests, for whose use the ceremonial weapons and garments were made. Priests needed knives no less than knights needed swords, for the Aztecs' bloodthirsty gods—especially Huitzilopochtli, the war god, and Tlaloc, god of rain—had to be fed on a plentiful supply of hearts ripped, still throbbing, from the breasts of human victims.

In the minds of the Aztecs, ritual was inextricably tied up with the calendar. They inherited the calendrical system of the Maya, which means that they recognized a solar year of 365 days, but geared their regularly recurring ritual occasions to a period of 260 days. The beginning of a solar year thus corresponded with the beginning of a new ritual period only once in every 52 years. The end of a 52-year cycle was regarded as a time of crisis, when the world might come to a sudden terrible end if the right ritual precautions were not immediately taken.

When such a cycle ended the temple pyramids were therefore usually reconstructed. The pyramid of Tenayuca, for example, was reconstructed and enlarged on five occasions, which are thought to mark the end of the cycles in A.D. 1299, 1351, 1403, 1455 and 1507. Such ritual enlargements were accompanied by human sacrifices on a colossal scale.

Temple pyramids—particularly the great pyramid of Huitzilopochtli—were the dominating feature of Tenochtitlán, but they were not the only noteworthy buildings. For the Aztecs' two supreme chieftains there were two-storey palaces of stone and aromatic wood built round great courtyards, and many priests and military knights had spacious villas of similar construction. But the rest of the city's buildings consisted mainly of the homes of artisans—small one- and two-room houses of mud brick. By about A.D. 1500 there may have been as many as 60,000 of these houses, and the total population of the city is thought to have approached half a million people.

Most of these lived on the original island which the Aztecs had settled two centuries earlier, the rest on smaller adjacent islands and mud flats that had since been occupied and developed. With its straight, well-built paved streets, its floating gardens made of mud strewn on wickerwork rafts, and its several natural islands interspersed with canals, Tenochtitlán was, as the Spaniards were soon to call it, the veritable Venice of the New World. And by that time the city was connected to the shores of Lake Texcoco by three long causeways, while two aqueducts had been built across the brackish lake to bring in water from a source three miles distant.

The running of the city alone, apart from dealings with the various tributary tribes, required—and had—an efficient administration. At its peak were two supreme chieftains, elected from the four military chiefs of the Aztecs, who were themselves elected by a great council. Both chiefs fulfilled a priestly function, one additionally concerning himself with internal affairs, the other with warfare and relations with other tribes. When the Spaniards first landed in Mexico the latter position was held by Montezuma; and since, in this role, he was responsible for negotiations with them, they wrongly believed him to be sole and absolute ruler of the Aztecs.

This fourteenth-century Mexican sacrificial knife is made of chalcedony, a form of quartz. One conquistador hinted that such knives were far from sharp enough for their grisly purpose.

The Spaniards, led by Hernán Cortes, arrived on Mexico's east coast in 1519, and in spite of attempts on both sides to avoid it, they and the Aztecs were soon at war. Although he had only some 500 soldiers with him, Cortes had advantages which far outweighed his inferiority in numbers. His horses, carrying armoured men, were a sight wholly new to the Aztecs, and as unnerving as real-life centaurs might be to us; and his razor-sharp steel swords were far superior to any Aztec weapons. At the same time their own wars of conquest rebounded on them, and their long-suffering but powerful neighbours, the Tlaxcalans, allied themselves with the Spaniards. In the face of such opposition the Aztecs were overwhelmed, and in 1521 Tenochtitlán was razed to the ground and the treasures from its stores were on their way to Spain.

Within ten years other Spaniards had ventured far to the south and found another civilization, in some ways more advanced than that of the Aztecs, though even more short-lived. This was the Inca civilization of Peru. At the time when the Aztecs were beginning their wars of conquest, there were a number of tribal kingdoms in Peru, of which the most powerful was that of the Chimú, to the south of the Gulf of Guayaquil. The Chimú had a capital at Chan Chan which covered 11 square miles (2,850 hectares). It comprised irrigated areas and reservoirs, and ten walled compounds, each occupied by a single clan. There skilled craftsmen produced excellent pottery, textiles and metalwork.

The prosperity of the Chimú was in marked contrast to the situation of the Incas, who lived farther south, around Cuzco, in a range of the Andes. In the early part of the fifteenth century A.D. they were struggling for survival against neighbouring tribes. Their recovery, and their elevation to an imperial power, was brought about during the reign of one man, Pachacutec Inca, who became king of the Incas in 1438. (The king bore the title *Inca*, and this name was in time also applied to his people and their civilization.) In 20 years he extended Inca control over a 600-mile (960-kilometre) length of the Peruvian highlands, and his son, Tupac Inca, went on to conquer the Chimú, most of the coast lands of Peru, northern Chile and parts of northwest Argentina. By the early sixteenth century the Incas had also conquered northern Ecuador, and so controlled an empire that reached 2,300 miles (3,680 kilometres) from north to south, and up to 400 miles (640 kilometres) from west to east.

Much of this territory was very difficult terrain to conquer, hold and administer, being rugged highland country 10,000 feet (3,050 metres) and more above sea level. The key to the Incas' success was the construction of two imperial highways—the Royal Road winding in zigzag fashion through the highlands, and another road following the coast—which were linked by a number of east-west roads. Building the highland road, 3,200 miles (5,120 kilometres) long, presented difficult engineering problems which the Incas overcame by sheer perseverance and ingenuity. They created terraces where there were

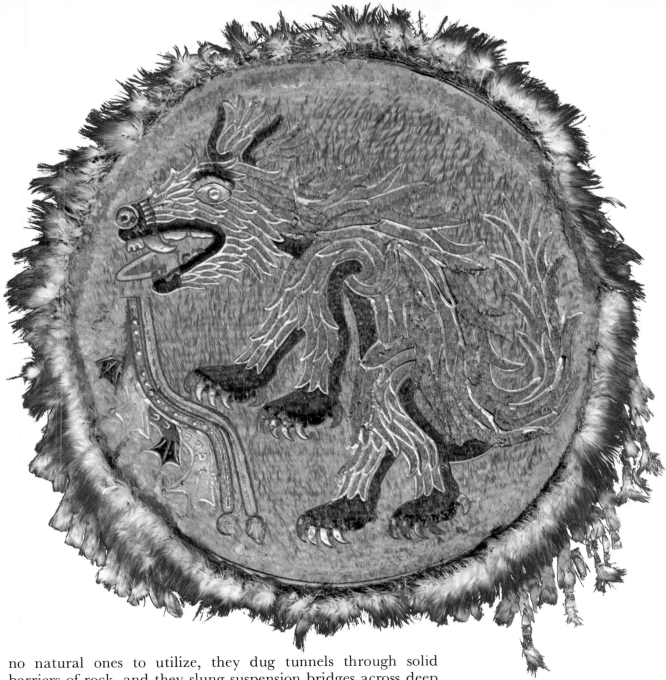

no natural ones to utilize, they dug tunnels through solid barriers of rock, and they slung suspension bridges across deep ravines. The shorter coastal road posed other problems. Here many rivers crossed the line of the road, and it had to be carried over them by pontoon bridges. Sand threatened to drift and cover the road in many places, and so it was bounded by walls on either side. But because no wheeled vehicle would travel the roads there was no need to provide them with good surfaces.

Like the Aztecs, the Incas had never seen a horse, but the imperial roads were nevertheless used not only for troop movements but also for a posting system. Messages were carried by men—with the stamina to run fast at high altitudes—housed in pairs in posting huts built along the roads. One man was always awake and ready to move. The services of these runners provided a vital link in the imperial administration, which was based on a series of provinces, each overseen by a governor. Governors received their orders from the Inca, who was assisted by advisers, and by a large civil service which exercised strict control over every aspect of life, from warfare and crime to marriage.

This feathered shield, given to Cortes in 1519, is the only one known to exist today. The Aztecs, who inherited the art of feather weaving from the Toltecs, sent merchants far and wide in search of brightly plumaged birds not to be found at the high altitude of Tenochtitlán.

So complex and all-pervading was state control that one might imagine it demanded a highly developed system of writing. Yet in this respect the Incas were not as well off as the Maya and Aztecs with their hieroglyphic scripts. The Incas had only the *quipu* to turn to. A quipu was a length of cord, about two feet (60 centimetres) long, from which many shorter, coloured threads were suspended. The colours represented certain objects or materials, and sometimes ideas as well. White thread, for example, could represent either silver or peace, while a red thread meant war. Knots tied in the threads represented numbers. It was possible, by various combinations of colours and knots, to record and convey a variety of information, and even to store it in archives, where archivists had to rely on their memories to fill in gaps that the quipus inevitably left.

As in all civilizations that demand a civil service and the keeping of records, it was essential to provide an education for at least an elite few. So at Cuzco, the Inca capital, there was a school where future leaders, priests and administrators were taught not only the art of reading quipus and keeping quipu archives but also military strategy and tactics, the rites of religion (which in Peru was centred mainly around the worship of the sun), and the laws of the empire.

Criminal laws were simple, and punishments usually severe. Theft, adultery and murder were all capital offences, although the death penalty was not imposed if there were mitigating cir-

Above: Inca travellers wind their way along the great imperial highway that zigzags through the highlands of South America for half the length of the continent. The llamas with them are the only animals they know of capable of carrying a light load, besides being the source of wool for much of their clothing. The map (right) shows the Inca Empire in A.D. 1500. It stretched northwards to beyond Quito, in modern Ecuador, and southwards to the Maule river, in central Chile. Its western frontier was the Pacific, its eastern frontier the fringe of the Amazon basin. Its great roads (red) were its links and lifelines.

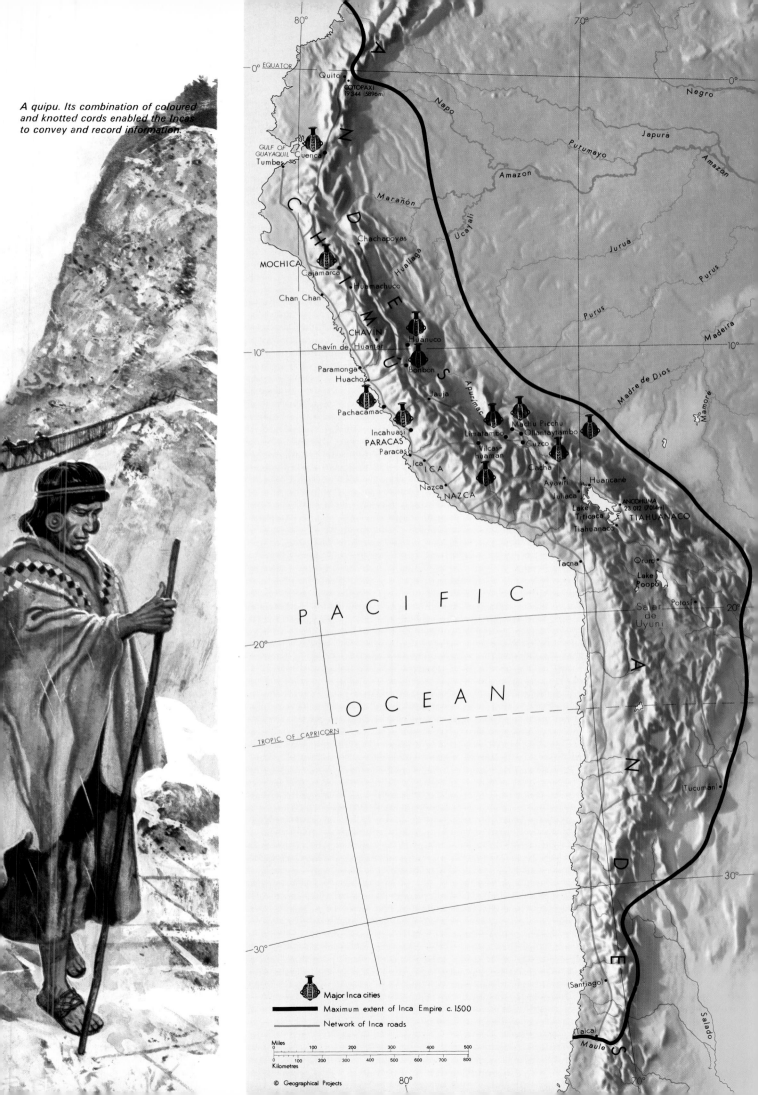

A quipu. Its combination of coloured and knotted cords enabled the Incas to convey and record information.

EQUATOR 0°

80° 70°

Negro

Quito

COTOPAXI
19.344 (5896m)

Napo

Putumayo

Japurá

Amazon

GULF OF
GUAYAQUIL
Tumbes

Cuenca

Marañón

Amazon

Chachapoyas

MOCHICA

Cajamarca

Huamachuco

Chan Chan

Huallaga

Ucayali

Juruá

Purús

Madeira

10°

CHAVÍN

Chavín de Huantar

Huánuco

Bonbon

Paramonga

Huachos

Jauja

Apurímac

Purús

Madre de Dios

Mamoré

Pachacamac

Incahuasi

PARACAS
Paracas

Ica

ICA

Nazca

NAZCA

Limatambo

Vilcas-
huamán

Machu Picchu

Ollantaytambo

Cuzco

Cacha

Ayaviri

Huancané

Juliaca

ANCOHUMA
23.012 (7014m)

TIAHUANACO

Lake
Titicaca

Tiahuanaco

Oruro

Lake
Poopó

Tacna

Potosí

Salar
de
Uyuni

20°

PACIFIC

OCEAN

TROPIC OF CAPRICORN

(Tucumán)

(Santiago)

30°

(Talca)

Maule

Major Inca cities

Maximum extent of Inca Empire c. 1500

Network of Inca roads

Miles
0   100   200   300   400   500
0   100 200 300 400 500 600 700 800
Kilometres

© Geographical Projects

80°

70°

cumstances. Arson, laziness and the appropriation of a neighbour's water supply were also serious offences. But we learn from the Spanish conquistadors that the Inca people were extremely honest, and rarely stole from one another.

Most of them were still peasant farmers, living in the countryside, but tending their own plots of land had to take second place to working on land owned by the state and the temples. In addition, men could be called from their homes at any time for work on the roads, in the silver mines, or with the army. Women were no less hard-worked than men. Besides helping in the fields, wives were expected to cook, keep house, brew alcoholic drinks, spin and weave llama or alpaca wool, and make clothes for their own families and for state employees too.

Yet state control had its brighter side. When a man was ill, or too old to work, the state ensured that his land was tilled by others. If he lived in an arid area, state-built canals and aqueducts would bring water to irrigate his crops. The Inca kings not only controlled their people but also provided for them.

They did not, however, attempt to create a society in which all were equal. Enjoying a considerably better standard of living than the peasants were the craftsmen who produced goldwork, silverwork, tapestries, stone vessels and sculptures, hand-shaped pottery and superbly inlaid wooden vessels. Even more important and privileged were the priests and administrators, while at the peak of Inca society was the king or Inca himself, both ruler and god, Son of the Sun.

The Inca lived in a luxurious palace, guarded by 2,000 soldiers, in his magnificent capital at Cuzco, high in the Andes. There paved streets and canalized water ran between temples, storehouses and the palace buildings, all overlooked by the imposing fortress of Sacsahuamán, which stood on a rocky

Far left: Chimú or Mochica ceremonial gold mask. Right: Handle of a Chimú ceremonial knife, representing a demi-god wearing a headdress of delicate gold filigree. Around A.D. 1400, the Chimú kingdom, with its many craftsmen skilled in pottery, textiles and metalwork, was far more powerful than that of the Incas. Yet soon the Incas were to conquer the Chimú kingdom, and hold it as part of their growing empire for a century; and it was the Incas who were to become famous throughout the Old World for their fine goldwork.

Left: Machu Picchu, an Inca fortress-town probably built as a defence against the jungle tribes of the Amazon basin. For long years after the Spanish conquest neither conqueror nor conquered ever mentioned it. Rediscovered only in 1911, it now stands almost as the Incas built it, its single massive stone gateway, its barracks, its palaces, its plain, severe homes for ordinary folk all but intact.

eminence above the city. This fortress was built of multisided stone blocks, some of them 20 feet (6 metres) in height, and so accurately worked and fitted together that they formed almost water-tight joints of tremendous strength.

Similar construction methods were used for the store depots and barracks that were built at regular intervals along the imperial roads for the use of troops on the move; for only the army could keep the empire intact, and everything was done to ensure its efficiency. Organized in battalions and companies and equipped with metal-tipped spears as well as star-headed stone maces, slings and bows, it was superior to any other army in the New World. But it was no match for the arms, armour and horses of invaders from across the seas.

In 1531 a small force of about 100 Spanish infantry and 60 cavalry arrived in Peru, led by Francisco Pizarro. The following year, by trickery, Pizarro seized the emperor and held him ransom for a room full of gold. When the ransom was paid, the emperor was executed. The real weakness of the Inca Empire now emerged, for without its divine ruler it was uncoordinated and powerless. Pizarro's small force was able to march south to Cuzco and seize the whole empire with little trouble. When the Incas did eventually revolt against the conquerors the Inca Empire had already become but a province of Spain.

The speed and violence of the Spanish conquest destroyed the civilizations of the Aztec and Inca peoples when neither was much more than a century old. It brought European civilization to the New World and from then on the cultures of the New World were dominated by the civilizations of the Old. Had the civilizations of the Aztec and Inca been allowed to flourish uninterrupted, as did the civilizations of the Old World in ancient times, who knows what heights of prosperity and invention they might have reached?

Epilogue

The story of civilization is the story of man's increasing ability to build on the achievements of those who have gone before him and to learn from those who live around him. All the civilizations described in this book had their roots firmly planted in the past. In some cases this is well known and easily seen. In Mesopotamia, Palestine, Greece and Italy, for example, archaeologists long ago demonstrated that the great civilizations of these regions were preceded by a long, and often slow, process of social and technological progress. In the case of Shang China, the Indus valley civilization, the Aztecs and the Incas it is only in comparatively recent years that excavations have begun to reveal the earlier phases of man's journey on the path to civilization.

Once civilization emerged, the process of learning from contemporaries in other lands was stimulated and grew, for civilization almost always brought not only improvements in transport and communication but also the need and the desire to exchange materials and ideas with other peoples. Nowhere is this better demonstrated than in the eastern Mediterranean and the Middle East, where between 2000 and 1000 B.C. Babylonians, Egyptians, Minoans, Mycenaeans, Hittites, Canaanites and others engaged in a complex trading system of which we still know only the broad outlines. Inseparable from the exchange of manufactured goods and raw materials was an exchange of ideas—about agriculture, metalworking, shipbuilding, weapons of war, calendrical systems, and all kinds of matters. Inevitably, some of the ideas that were borrowed were improved on by the borrowers, who could look at them from a different viewpoint, or needed to apply them in a different way.

The classic illustration of this process is the development of writing. The Phoenicians, having become acquainted with both cuneiform and hieroglyphic scripts, developed alphabetic writing. The Greeks took up the idea and put it to more extensive use with the help of papyrus, a writing material that came from Egypt. From Greece this convenient method of writing was passed on to the Romans who adapted it to their own language, Latin, which was used from one end of the empire to the other, including regions such as emerging western Europe.

The Romans, of course, *imposed* their civilization—which owed so much to earlier ones—on Europe, but the imposition was both welcome and lasting. Throughout the comparatively chaotic three centuries that followed the final collapse of the Western Empire, some benefits of the Roman occupation were still felt in western Europe—benefits such as the road system and the use of Latin among the educated. At the same time the accumulated knowledge of the ancient world was preserved in the former Eastern Empire, now the Byzantine Empire, together with the invaluable writings of both Greek and Latin authors; and all this was to reemerge when Europe finally shook off its self-imposed barbarism in the early Middle Ages. Thus, in the civilization of Medieval Europe we find much that was first introduced to the continent by the Romans. Latin, for example, was still the *lingua franca*; the Julian calendar remained in use in most of Europe until 1582 and in Britain until 1752; many names for months and days were, and still are, Roman names; in much of Europe Roman law was, and still is, the basis for national law. And if one looks at a map of modern Europe and picks out the major cities, most of them will be found to be on the sites of Roman ones, including important capitals such as London, Paris, Rome and Bonn.

The debt of modern European civilization to that of Rome is thus considerable, and pervades many different aspects of life. Indirectly the debt is extended to those parts of the world where Europeans conquered or settled, and this, of course, covers much of the globe. But as Europeans spread their own civilization, they also learned much from the cultures, and sometimes the civilizations, of those they conquered.

In our own time, with even faster and more effective means of communication, man can share ideas, ideals and experiences with his fellow man the world over more rapidly and more intimately than ever before. What he is making of his opportunities determines the present state of civilization. And with every moment that passes that present is slipping back into the past on which future generations will build.

Index

References in *italics* are to illustrations or captions to illustrations. References in **bold** are to maps or captions to maps.

A

Abu Simbel, Egypt: fortress, **31**; temple, 32

administration, 15; Aztec, 115; Chinese, 55; Inca, 116–18, 120; Roman, 107; of Western Asian empires, 79, 80–1, 83

Aegean civilizations, 84–95

Aeschylus, dramatist, 92

Afghanistan, metals from, 47

Africa: Phoenician circumnavigation of, 69–70; Roman province in, 99

agora, Greek marketplace, *84–5*, 94

Akhenaton, pharaoh, 32

Akhetaton, capital of Akhenaton, 36, *37*

Akkadian Empire, *21*

Alcmaeon, physician, 91

Alexander the Great, 75–6, 83, 84, 89; empire of, **94–5**

alphabetic script, Phoenician, 71, *71*, 123

Amarna letters, 36, 38

America, early civilizations of, 110–21

amphitheatres, Roman, 105; gladiators in, *107*

Amurru (Amorites), 22, 49

anatomy, Greek knowledge of, 91

Anaxagoras, philosopher, 91

ancestor worship, China, 53

animals: domestication of, 11, 13, 18; hunting of, 10; sacrifices of (China), 56; selective breeding of, 14

An-yang, Shang capital, 56; burial chambers at, 56–7

aqueducts: Aztec, 115; Inca, 120; Roman, *102–3*, 104

Aramaic language, in Persian Empire, 80

arches, building of, 23

architecture: Egyptian, 30; Greek, 95; Inca, 121; Minoan, 63–4; Roman, 103; Western Asian, 76–7; *see also* houses, temples

Aristophanes, dramatist, 92, 93

Aristotle, philosopher, 92

armies: Egyptian, 36; Inca, 121; Macedonian, 89; Mesopotamian, 22–3; Persian, *78–9*; Roman, 100–2; Shang, 55

armour: Greek, *87*; Roman, *96–7*

arrowheads: bronze, *56–7*; stone, *10*

Artaxerxes III of Persia, 75

arts, 13, 15; in Crete, 65; in Egypt, 30, 40; in Greece, 89; in Mesopotamia, 27

Aryans, invade India, 49

Asia Minor: Cretan trade with, 65; Greeks flee to, 84, **86–7**; southeast, early farmers in, 16; western, as Roman province, 99

Assurbanipal of Assyria, 27, 75, 82

Assurnasirpal II of Assyria, 72

Assyria, 22; Assyrian Empire, 72–3, **74–5**, 75, 77; and subject peoples, 83

astronomy: Chaldean (neo-Babylonian), 82; Egyptian, 39; Mesopotamian, 25

Athens, *78–9*, *84–5*, 88

athletics, Greek, 90, *90–1*

augurs, in China, 53

axes: Aryan shaft-hole, 49; Egyptian socketed, *36*; Mesopotamian narrow-bladed, *22–3*

Aztecs, 113–15; empire of, **113**; war party of, with captives, *110–11*

B

Babylon, 75, *76–7*

Babylonian Empire, 22, 72

Bahrain, on trade routes, 47

Baluchistan, bronze from? 48, *49*

banks, Persian, 81

barley, 13, 14; in Indus valley, 45

baths, Roman, 104, *106*

beans, in Mexico, 110

bellows: invention of, 40; Chinese piston, 58

Black Sea, Greek colonies round, 87

boats and ships; Egyptian, *28–9*, 35–6; Mesopotamian, 24; Persian, 81–2; Phoenician, *66–7*, 69

botanical gardens, Western Asia, 82

bow and arrows: in hunting, 10; in warfare, 22, 36, 55, *57*, 78

bricks: fired, of Indus valley, 45, and of Rome and Egypt, 103; mud, of Mesopotamia, 18, *18*

British Isles, Phoenician voyage to, 70

bronze, 40, 47, 48–9, *49*, 60; Chinese, 52, *52–3*, *58*; Greek, 90; multiple-mould casting of, 24, *50–1*, 53, 58

Bronze Age, 67; Aegean in, **62–3**; empires of, 72

bull game, Crete, *65*

Byblos, Phoenicia, *28*, 67

Byzantine Empire, 100, 109, *109*, 123

C

Cádiz, Phoenician colony, 69

calendar: Aztec, 114–15; Egyptian, 39; Julian, 123; Mayan, 112

Cambyses of Persia, 75

Canaanites, 68

canals, in Mesopotamia, 24, 81

Carthage, Phoenician colony, 69–71; Rome and, 99

cattle, domesticated, *46–7*, 57

cave paintings, 11, 13, *14–15*; distribution of, **15**

cedar forests, Phoenicia, 67

cereals, wild, 13, 14, *16–17*, 18

Chaldean (Neo-Babylonian) Empire, 72, 75

Chan Chan, Chimú capital, 116

chariots: Chinese, 55, *57*; Egyptian, 36, *36*; Mesopotamian, 22, *22–3*

chemistry, Assyrian, 82

Cheng-chou, Shang capital, 56

Cheops, pharaoh, 32, *32*

Chimú people, Peru, 116, *120–1*

Ch'in Dynasty, China, 58; territory of, **59**

China, Great Plain of: civilization in, 16, 50–9

Chinese characters, 53, 55, *55*

Chou Dynasty, China, 57, 58; territory of, **59**

Christianity, Constantine and, 109

Cicero, advocate and author, 108, 109

Circus Maximus, Rome, 105

citadels, of Indus valley cities, *44–5*, 45, 46

cities: in Assyria, **74–5**; in China, 56; in Egypt, **31**; in Greece, 94–5; of Incas, **119**; in Indus valley, 44–5; Mayan, **113**; in Mesopotamia, 18, 21, **22**, 23; in Phoenicia, **66–7**, 69

city-states: Greek, 84, **86–7**, 87–8; Mesopotamian, 21; Phoenician, 68

civilization: definition of, 15–16; earliest sites of development of, **12–13**, 16

clocks, Egyptian sand and water, 40

cloth, purple-dyed Phoenician, 69

coins: Lydian, 81; Persian archers, *80–1*

colleges, Egyptian priestly, 38

colonies: Assyrian, **74–5**; Cretan, 65; Greek, 84, **86–7**, 87, 96, **98–9**; Phoenician, 69, **70–1**, 87

concrete, Roman use of, 103

Constantine, emperor, 100, 109

Constantinople, 100

copper, 47; pottery glaze containing, 30; tools of, *22–3*, 30, 45

Cortes, Hernán, Spanish conqueror, 116, *117*

cotton, at Mohenjo-daro, 45

crafts, specialist, 15–16, 21; Aztec, 114; Chinese, 56; Inca, 120; Mesopotamian, 26–7; Phoenician, 68

Crassus, Roman ruler, 99

Craterus, commander under Alexander, **94–5**

Crete, civilization of, 60–6

Croesus of Lydia, 81

crops: in Indus valley, 46; introduced by Persians, 81; in Mesopotamia, 18; in Mexico, 110; in Roman Empire, 103

crucibles, heat-retaining (China), 53, 58

cuneiform characters, *24*, 25, 38, 82

Cuzco, Inca capital, 118, 120

cylinder seals, Mesopotamia, *24*, 25

Cyprus, Cretan trade with, 65

Cyrus the Great of Persia, 75, 81

D

Darius the Great of Persia, 75, *80–1*, 82
Darius III of Persia, 76
dates, grown in Indus valley, 45
deforestation, Indus valley, 49
Delphi, theatre at, *92–3*
Democedes, physician, 91
democracy, in Athens, 88, 92
Democritus, philosopher, 91
demotic characters, 38
deserts: bordering Egypt, 28, *30–1*;
    raiders from, **20–1**, 21–2, **36–7**
Diocletian, emperor, 100
diplomacy, profession of, 26
donkeys, transport by, 24
Dorians, invade Greece, 84, **86–7**
drainage systems: in Indus valley cities,
    45; in Palace of Knossos, 64
drama, Greek, 92–3, *92–3*

E

earthquakes, in Crete, 60
eclipses, Assyrian records of, 82
Egypt, 16, 17, 28–41, 72; trades with
    Crete, 65; under Assyria, 75
Epicharmus, dramatist, 92
Etruscans, 87, 96
Euphrates, 18, **20–1**; Egypt reaches to,
    30
excavations, knowledge obtained by, 122
Eynan (Palestine), early farmers at,
    14, 15

F

Faiyum, 28
farmers, 13–14, 15, 16; in China, 50, 52;
    in Egypt, 28; in Mesopotamia, 18;
    in Mexico, 110; in Roman Empire, 103
feather work: of Aztecs, *116*; of Toltecs,
    113
Fertile Crescent, **20–1**, 75
feudalism, Chinese, 53, 55
fire, use of, 10

G

game with board and pieces,
    Mesopotamia, *27*

Gilgamesh, Epic of, 27
Giza, pyramids at, 32, *32*
glass vessels, Phoenician, 68, *69*
goats, domesticated, 13, 14, *16–17*, 18,
    50
goldwork: Chimú and Inca, 110, 112,
    120–1; Cretan, 60; Mesopotamian, 24;
    Phoenician, *71*
granaries: in China, 52; in Indus valley,
    45, 46, *46–7*; in Roman forts, 102
grave offerings, 13; at An-yang (horses
    and chariot), 56–7, *58*; in Egypt,
    40–1; at Mycenae, 84
Great Wall of China, 58, **59**
Greeks, 84–95; use Phoenician
    alphabet, 71
gymnasium, Greek, 95

H

Hadrian's Wall, Britian, *96–7*
halberds, 52, 55, *56*, 57
Hammurabi of Babylonia, 22, *24–5*, 26
Han Dynasty, China, 58
Hannibal, Carthaginian general, 99
Hanno of Carthage, 70
Harappa, Indus valley, 45, 49
harness for horses, Chinese and, 58
harp, Mesopotamian, *26*, 27
Herodotus, historian, 70, 93
hieratic characters, 38
hieroglyphic characters, 123; Egyptian,
    30–1, 38, *38*, 39; of Maya people,
    64; of Minoans, 64
Himilco, Carthaginian general, 70
Hindu religion, 49
Hippocrates of Kos, physician, 91
Hippodamus of Miletus, architect, 94
Hittites, 22; Hittite Empire, 72
Homer, poet, 87
Homo erectus, 10
Homo habilis, 8
Homo sapiens modernis, 13
Horace, poet, 108
houses: in China, 50, 56; of early man,
    (shelters) *8–9*, 10, (huts) 15; in
    Indus valley, 45; in Mesopotamia, 23;
    of Romans, 106, *108–9*; in
    Tenochtitlán, 115
human sacrifice: by Aztecs, 114, *114*,
    115; in China, 56
hunting, 10; organized, 11
Hwang Ho, 50
Hyksos, invade Egypt, 30, **36–7**, 49

I

icecaps of Ice Age, extent of, **12–13**
ideas, exchange of, 8, 13, 66, 122

Imhotep, builder of pyramids, 32
Incas, 116–18, 120–1; empire of, **119**
Indus river, 42
Indus valley civilization, 16, 42–9
iron: Chinese cast, 58; used by Dorians,
    84; welding of, 91
Iron Age, empires of, 72
irrigation, 16, 18; in Egypt, 30; in
    Indus valley, 46; at Jericho, 15; in
    Mesopotamia, 18, 21; in Mexico, 110
Ishtar Gate, Babylon, *76–7*, 77
Isocrates, teacher, 92
Israelites, 68
ivory, Phoenician carvings in, 68, *68*

J

Jehu of Israel, 72
Jericho, 14, 15, *17*
jewellery: Aztec, 114; Cretan, 60;
    Egyptian, *41*; Indian, 45;
    Mesopotamian, 24
Jews, allowed by Persians to return
    home from exile, 81
Julius Caesar, 99–100, 108
Justinian, emperor, *109*

K

Kalibangan, Indus valley, 45
Kassite tribesmen, 22
Karnak, temple of Amun-Ra at, *34–5*, 35
kings: emergence of, 23, 52; of Shang
    Dynasty, 52, 53
knives: Aztec sacrificial, *115*; Chimú
    cerémonial, *121*
Knossos, palace at, 60, *60–1*, *63*, 63–4,
    64

L

Lascaux, cave painting at, *14–15*
lathe, invention of, 91
Latin language, 109, 123
laws, 16, 21; Egyptian, 38–9; of
    Hammurabi, *24–5*, 26; Inca, 118;
    Roman, 107–8, 123
lead, in Chinese bronze, 53
legions, Roman, 101
Leptis Magna (North Africa), Roman
    bath at, *106*

libraries: in Nineveh, 82; in Rome, 108
Linear A and Linear B scripts, 63, 64
literature: Egyptian, 40; Greek, 71, 89, 91; Mesopotamian, 27; Roman, 108–9
Livy, historian, 108
llamas, *118–19*
loess soil, China, 50
Lydia, Asia Minor, 75, 81

Macedonia, 89; as Roman province, 99
Machu Picchu, Inca fortress-town, *120–1*
maize, in Mexico, 110
mammoths, 10; shelter made from tusks and skins of, *8–9*
man: characteristics of, 8; time chart of development of, *10*
Marathon, Battle of, 75, 84, 88
masks: Chimú ceremonial gold, *120–1*; comic and tragic, of Greek drama, *92–3*; prehistoric antler, 13, *14–15*
mathematics: Egyptian, 38, 39; Mayan, 112–13; Mesopotamian, 25
Maximian, emperor, 100
Maya people, 112–113; extent of culture of, **113**
Medes, 75, *79*
medicine: Egyptian, 40; Greek, 91; Mesopotamian, 26
melons, in Indus valley, 45
Mesopotamia, 16, 18–27; contacts of Indus valley with, 42, 45, 47
metal working, 16; in China, *50–1*, *52–3*; in Crete, 60; in Egypt, 40; in Indus valley, 48; in Mesopotamia, 21, 24
metals, 46–7, 65; alloys of, 24; imported into Indus valley, 46–7, and Mesopotamia, 21, 23; in Peru, 110–11
Mexico, early farming in, 110, 112
Miletus, planning of, 94
millet, in China, 50, 52
Minoan civilization, 60, **62–3**, **64**; Mycenaeans and, 84; *see also* Crete
Mithraism, 81
Mohenjo-daro, Indus valley, *42–3*, 45, 46
Montezuma, Aztec chieftain, 115
Motya (Sicily), Phoenician colony, 69
mountains: early farmers in, 18; raiders from, **20–1**
mummification, 40, *40–1*
Murex, mollusc yielding purple dye, 69
museum, at Babylon, 82
music: Egyptian, 40; Mesopotamian, 27
Mycenae, 84
Mycenaean civilization, **62–3**, 63, 66, 84, 87
Myron, sculptor, 90

Narmer of Egypt, slate palate of, *30–1*
navies: Athenian, *78–9*, 88; Egyptian, 35–6; Persian, 82
Neanderthal man, *10*, 13
Nearchus, commander under Alexander, **94–5**
Nebuchadnezzar II of Babylon, 75, 82
Nile, 28, *30–1*; labour force required for controlling floods of, 32
Nineveh, 75, 76
Nubians, **36–7**
number systems of Mesopotamia, decimal and sexagesimal, 25

oats, 103
obsidian, 35; used for Aztec knife blades, 114
Octavian, emperor, *99*, 100
olive oil, exported from Crete, 65
Olympic Games, 90, *90–1*
Olynthus, planning of, 94
oracles, in China, 53, *55*

Pachacutec Inca, 116
paintings, *see* cave paintings, vase paintings, wall paintings
Palestine, early farmers in, 13, 14, 15, 16
papyrus, 38, *39*, 108, 123
Papyrus of Ani, *38–9*
parchment, books written on, 108
Parthenon, Athens, *88–9*, 90, *94–5*
Peloponnesian War, 88, 92
"Peoples of the Sea," 35, **36–7**
Pericles, statesman, 88, 90
Persepolis, 76, 77, *82–3*
Persia (Iran), and Indus valley, 42, **44–5**
Persian Empire, 72, 75–6, 77, **80–1**, 83
Peru, 110, 116
pharaohs, 30, 40
Phidias, sculptor, *88–9*, 90
Philip of Macedonia, 89
Philistines, 68
philosophy, Greek, 84–5, 91, 92
Phoenicia, **67**

Phoenicians, 66–71; as crews for Persian ships, 82
pigs, domesticated in China, 50
Piraeus, port of Athens, 94
pistachio nut, Persians and, 81
Pizarro, Francisco, Spanish conqueror, 121
plants: domestication of, 13; selective breeding of, 14
Plataea, Battle of, 75
Plato, philosopher, 92
Pliny the Younger, advocate and author, 108
ploughing, 18, 45
Pompey, Roman ruler, 99, 100
Pomponius, organizes copying of books, 109
Pont du Gard, aqueduct, *102–3*
populations: increased after Ice Age, 13; of Nineveh and Babylon, 76; of Tenochtitlán, 115
posting systems: Inca, 117; Roman, 103
potter's wheel, 50
pottery: Chinese, 50; Egyptian, 30; Greek, *88*, 89; Indian, *48*; Minoan, 65; Roman, 103
Priene, planning of, 94
priests: Aztec, 115; Egyptian, 40; Mesopotamian, 21, 23
Protagoras, philosopher, 91
Punic Wars, 99
pyramids: Aztec, 115; Egyptian, 32, *32–3*, 35, 39; Mayan, 112
Pyrrhus of Epirus, 96
Pythagoras, 91; theorem of, 25

quipu, Inca method of recording information, 118, *118–19*

Ramses II, pharaoh, 32
reindeer, economy based on, 10–11
religion, 13; Assyrian and Babylonian tolerance in matters of, 81; Aztec, 114–15; Chinese, 53; Egyptian, 40; Inca, 118; Indus valley, 49; Mesopotamian, 21, 23, 27
rhetoric, 92
rice, Persians and, 81
Rigveda, Indian hymns, 49

roads: Assyrian, 79–80; Inca, 116–17, *118–19*, **119**; Persian, 80, **80–1**; Roman, **98–9**, *100–1*, 102–3, **104–5**
Romans, 71, 81, 95; civilization of, 96–109; empire of, **104–5**
rye, 103

Sacsahuamán, Inca fortress, 120–1
Sakkara, pyramid at, 32
Salamis, Battle of, 75, *78–9*, 84
Sardis, road from Susa to, **80–1**
Sargon of Akkadia, 21, *21*
satrapies of Persian Empire, 80–1, **80–1**
scarab beetle, *41*
school exercises, on Mesopotamian tablets, 25
science, Greek, 91
sculpture: Assyrian, 77; Greek, *89*, 89–90; Indian, *49*; Mayan, 112; Mesopotamian, 27; Persian, *82–3*; Roman, *104*; Toltec, *112*
seals: Indian, *46–7*, 49; Mesopotamian cylinder, *24*, 25
Senate, Roman, 99
sesame: in Indus valley, 45; Persians and, 81
Shalmaneser III of Assyria, 72
Shang Dynasty, China, 52
Shang kingdom, 53, **54–5**, 55–7
Shanidar (Iran), early farmers at, 13, 15
sheep, domesticated, 13, 14, *16–17*, 18
ships, *see* boats and ships
Sicily: Phoenician colonies in, 69; as Roman province, 99
sickles, Chinese store of, 52
siege warfare, 36; Assyrian, *72–3*, 78–9
silk, in China, 52
silver bowls, Phoenician, 68
slaves: of Aztecs, 114; labour of, in Roman Empire, 103; owned by Egyptian temple, 40
social stratification, 16
Socrates, philosopher, 91–2
Solomon of Israel, 68
Sophocles, dramatist, 92
"sorcerer," with antler mask, 13, *14–15*
Spaniards, conquests of: Aztecs, 115–16; Incas, 121
Sparta, 88
spearheads, socketed, 52, *56–7*
spears: in hunting, 10; in warfare, 22, 36, *87*, 121
spear thrower, 10, *11*
speech, development of, 8
stone: in Egypt, 32, 35; imported into Mesopotamia, 23; tools of, 8, 10, *10*
Sumerians, *22–3*; *see also* Mesopotamia
Susa, 26, 76, 82; road to Sardis from, **80–1**
swimming pool, at Mohenjo-daro, 46

Tacitus, historian, 108
temples: Egyptian, **31**, *34–5*, 35, 40; Greek, *88–9*, 90, 94, *94–5*; Mesopotamian (ziggurats), 18, *18–19*, **22**, 23
Tenochtitlán, Aztec capital, 113, 114, 115; destroyed by Spaniards, 116
theatres: Greek, *92–3*, 94–5; Roman, 105
Thera island, destroyed by volcanic eruption, 63
Thucydides, historian, 93–4
Thutmosis III of Egypt, 30
Tiglath Pileser III of Assyria, 72, 79
Tigris, 18, **20–1**
timber: in Crete, **65**; imported into Egypt, *28*, 35, 67, and into Mesopotamia, 23
tin, 47, 53, 70
Toltec people, *112–13*, 113
tools: bronze, 60; copper, *22–3*, 30, 45; stone, 8, 10, *10*; storehouse of (China), 52
town planning: Greece, 94–5; Indus valley, 45
towns, 15, 16; *see also* cities
trade, 16, 122; of Crete, 65, 66; of Egypt, 35; of Indus valley, *46–7*, 49; of Mesopotamia, 21, 23–4, 26; of Mycenae, 84; of Phoenicia, 67, 69, 71
trade routes, 67; Indus valley, **48**; Mesopotamian, 24; Minoan, *62–3*, **70**; Phoenician, **70**
triremes, *78–9*
Troy, war between Mycenae and, 87, 96
Tupac Inca, 116
Tutankhamen of Egypt, tomb of, *40–1*

Ugarit (Syria), 67
Ur, Mesopotamian city, *18–19*, 21, 23; Indus valley seals found in, 47
Urartu kingdom, Asia Minor, 72

vase paintings, Greek, *88*, 89
vegetables, grown by Romans, 103
Vergil, poet, 108
vines, in Crete, 65
Visigoths, sack Rome, 100

Vitruvius, architect, 108
vizier, in Egypt, 39
volcanic eruption on Thera island, and Crete, 63

wagon, Indus valley ox-drawn, *46–7*
wall paintings (frescoes): Mayan, 112; Minoan, *63*, 63–4, 65
walls of cities: China, 56; Indus valley, 45; Jericho, *11*; Mesopotamia, 23
warfare, 11; Assyrian, 77–9; Egyptian, 30, 35–6; Mesopotamian, 22–3
warring states period, China, 57–8, **59**
watermill, used by Romans, 103
weights and measures, 16; Egyptian law on falsification of, 38; in Indus valley, 47–8; in Persia, 81
wheat, 13, 14; in China, 52; in Indus valley, 45
wheel, invention of, 24
wine, exported from Crete, 65
writing, 16, 21, 123; in China, 53; in Crete, 63; in Egypt, 38; in Indus valley, not yet deciphered, 46; in Mesopotamia, 25–6

Xerxes of Persia, 75, 77, *78–9*

Yucatan, 112, *113*

Zagros Mountains (Iran), early farmers in, 13, 18
ziggurats, Mesopotamia, 18, *18–19*, **22**, 23
zoological gardens, Western Asia, 82
Zoroaster, prophet, 81

Acknowledgements

Page 7 Quotation from *The Bleak Age*, J. L. and Barbara Hammond, revised edition, Pelican Books, 1947: Page 10(B) Kenneth P. Oakley, *Man the Toolmaker*/British Museum (Natural History): Page 14(T) Popperfoto: Page 14(B) Aldus Archives: Page 17(R) Dame Kathleen Kenyon: Page 21(R) Giraudon: Page 23(T) Reproduced by permission of the Trustees of the British Museum: Page 23(B) Michael Holford Library photo: Page 24(L) Reproduced by permission of the Trustees of the British Museum: Page 25 Photo André Vigneau © Editions Tel: Page 26 Reproduced by permission of the Trustees of the British Museum: page 30(B) Hirmer Fotoarchiv Munich: Page 31(L) Roger Wood, London: Page 34 Professor Kazimierz Michalowski, *l'Art de l'Ancienne Egypte*, Editions d'Art Lucien Mazenod, Paris/Photo Jean Vertut: Page 38(B) Ardea, London: Pages 39(T), 40(T) Michael Holford Library photo: Page 41(R) Photos F. L. Kenett © George Rainbird Ltd.: Page 46(B) Robert Harding Associates: Page 47(B) Rapho: Pages 48(T), 49 Robert Harding Associates: Pages 52–3 Robert Harding Associates: Page 55(TC) Robert Harding Associates: Page 56 Government of China/Robert Harding Associates: Page 58(T) Britain-China Friendship Association: Page 58(B) Robert Harding Associates: Page 63(R) Hirmer Fotoarchiv Munich: Page 64(T) Keith Branigan: Pages 68–9 Reproduced by permission of the Trustees of the British Museum: Page 71(T) Michael Holford Library photo: Page 77(B) Staatliche Museen, Berlin: Page 80(B) British Museum/Photos Eileen Tweedy © Aldus Books: Page 82(B) Roger Wood, London: Page 88 British Museum/Photos Eileen Tweedy © Aldus Books: Page 89 Michael Holford Library photo: Page 92(T) Robert Harding Associates: Page 92(C) Staatliche Museen, Berlin: Page 92(B) British Museum/Photo Eileen Tweedy © Aldus Books: Page 95 Werner Forman Archive: Page 99 Kunsthistorisches Museum, Wien: Page 102 Picturepoint, London: Page 104(L) The Mansell Collection: Page 106 Roger Wood, London: Pages 108–9 Scala, Florence: Page 112 Werner Forman Archive: Page 114 British Museum/Photo John Freeman © Aldus Books: Page 115 Reproduced by permission of the Trustees of the British Museum: Page 116 Museum für Völkerkunde, Wien: Page 118(TR) Courtesy of The American Museum of Natural History: Pages 120–1 Robert Harding Associates.